ARCHITECTURE

Practical Applications

Also in this series:

(Practical Applications)
Agriculture
Art
Education
Medicine
Religion
Science
Social and Political Science

(Esoteric)
Alchemy
Atlantis
Christian Rozenkreutz
The Druids
The Goddess
The Holy Grail

RUDOLF STEINER

ARCHITECTURE
An Introductory Reader

Compiled with an introduction, commentary and notes by Andrew Beard

Sophia Books

All translations revised by Matthew Barton

Sophia Books
An imprint of Rudolf Steiner Press
Hillside House, The Square
Forest Row, RH18 5ES

www.rudolfsteinerpress.com

Published by Rudolf Steiner Press 2003

For earlier English publications of individual selections please see pp. 265–6

The material by Rudolf Steiner was originally published in German in various volumes of the 'GA' (*Rudolf Steiner Gesamtausgabe* or Collected Works) by Rudolf Steiner Verlag, Dornach. This authorized volume is published by permission of the Rudolf Steiner Nachlassverwaltung, Dornach (for further information see pp. 273–4)

This selection and translation © Rudolf Steiner Press 2003

All rights reserved. No part of this publication may be reproduced, stored in a retrieval system, or transmitted, in any form or by any means, electronic, mechanical, photocopying or otherwise, without the prior permission of the publishers

A catalogue record for this book is available from the British Library

ISBN 1 85584 123 1

Cover by Andrew Morgan Design
Typeset by DP Photosetting, Aylesbury, Bucks.
Printed and bound in Great Britain by Cromwell Press Limited, Trowbridge, Wilts.

Contents

Introduction *by Andrew Beard* — 1

Part One

1. The Origins and Nature of Architecture — 19
2. The Formative Influence of Architecture on the Human Being — 28
3. The History of Architecture in the Light of Mankind's Spiritual Evolution — 37
4. A New Architecture as a Means of Uniting with Spiritual Forces — 54
5. Art and Architecture as Manifestations of Spiritual Realities — 77
6. Metamorphosis in Architecture — 97
7. Aspects of a New Architecture — 125
8. Rudolf Steiner on the First Goetheanum Building — 148
9. The Second Goetheanum Building — 184
10. The Architecture of a Community in Dornach — 192

Part Two
The Temple Legend: underlying esoteric aspects of Steiner's vision

11. The Temple is the Human Being — 213
12. The Restoration of the Lost Temple — 234

Notes	253
Sources	265
Bibliography	267
Further Reading	269
Illustration Credits	271
Note Regarding Rudolf Steiner's Lectures	273

Introduction

By Andrew Beard

The contents of this book are drawn mainly from lectures given at different times and places between 1905 and 1924. They are assembled under what I hope are useful headings, allowing the reader to navigate through a landscape with many different features.

Part One begins with Steiner's understanding of the nature and origins of architecture. From there it moves to a discussion of how architectural forms affect and influence the human being and how this influence has accompanied mankind's cultural development. Chapters 4–7 are concerned with Steiner's view of the spiritual dimension of architecture and its task in our present age, particularly his interest in finding architectural expression for processes of metamorphic change and evolution. In chapters 8–10 Steiner talks directly about his two major architectural works, the first and second Goetheanum buildings and the community of buildings around them.

Part Two is based on the Temple Legend, relating to the origins of human life on earth and containing an image of the human being as a temple in which the divinity is represented by the human 'I' or ego. According to this legend the future of humanity depends on recovering and restoring the lost 'temple' of the human body and the earth.

Rudolf Steiner and the modern movement in art and architecture

Rudolf Steiner's architectural work can be seen in the context of the pioneering days of modern architecture. His active period as an architect, from around 1907 to 1924 coincides with landmark buildings by Walter Gropius, Le Corbusier and Frank Lloyd Wright, among others. Most historians who have sought to place his work have identified connections with an earlier generation of art nouveau artists and designers such as Victor Horta in Belgium, Charles Rennie Mackintosh in Scotland and others. Steiner's work has also been seen as part of the expressionist stream whose members can be said to include Antonio Gaudi, Saint Elia, Herman Finsterlin, the earlier work of Erich Mendelsohn, Hans Scharoun and Eero Saarinen. Steiner's Goetheanum buildings could be seen as built examples of the 'Volkhaus' (house of the people) or 'Stadtkrone' (city crown) advocated by Bruno Taut, among others, as cultural centres representing secular versions of the medieval cathedral.[1] Other, more recent names could be added to the list of architects whose work includes expressionist elements, such as the American Frank Gehry, who built the well-known Guggenheim Museum in Bilbao, the Hungarian Imre

Makovecz, the Spanish architect Santiago Calatrava and recent work by the Italian Renzo Piano, co-designer of the 'high-tech' Centre Pompidou in Paris.

As time goes on, however, it is possible that Steiner's work may be seen in a broader context than art nouveau, which preceded it, and early expressionism with which it coincided. In common with all the pioneers of modern art and architecture Steiner railed against the degeneracy of most nineteenth-century architecture, with its eclectic plagiarism of former styles. Our present age, he believed, requires a complete renewal of all the arts,[2] a renewal, however, based on a return to the fundamental principles inherent in art and architecture which find expression through different ages and cultures. For example, the Swiss-French architect Le Corbusier was inspired by the archetypal quality of ancient Greek architecture and its use of the laws of proportion, inherent in the human body and reproduced in the ordering of architectural space and forms. The resonance which Le Corbusier experienced between the proportion of the 'golden section' and the human body should not be dismissed as a whim. As he put it, 'Mathematica (is) herself the daughter of the universe.'[3]

Le Corbusier is one example of an architect who is not necessarily thought of as working from a spiritual perspective. However, the spiritual dimension embraced by many pioneers of twentieth-century art and design is now becoming better known and understood. Kandinsky's essay *Concerning the Spiritual in Art* is a well-known example, but there are many others.[4]

4 ARCHITECTURE

Detail of the second Goetheanum building begun in 1925 by Rudolf Steiner

Introduction 5

TWA airline terminal at JFK Airport New York, by Eero Saarinen, 1956–62

6   ARCHITECTURE

Le Corbusier's 'Modulor Man', as he became known, showing the relationship between the human body and the proportions of the 'golden section'.

A more direct connection can be argued between Steiner's architectural work and the so-called 'organic' stream. In the sense that organic architecture is inspired by natural forms, particularly plant forms, comparisons can be made between art nouveau buildings and Steiner's first Goetheanum. Steiner's interest in morphology, however, went beyond the outer appearance of natural forms and was more concerned with the laws according to which forms come into being. This particular interest was shared by the Chicago architect Louis Sullivan, who was responsible for the aphorism 'Form follows function'. This expression has been interpreted in different ways by different architects but Steiner would have said that form is a direct outcome of the activity it supports and the context in which it arises, without any preconceptions by the designer, including a pre-conceived style. In this sense 'organic architecture' does not so much involve imitating the external appearance of natural forms but getting inside nature's skin and applying her methods to produce a unique solution to each problem. Here, Steiner can be placed alongside masters like Frank Lloyd Wright, Alvar Aalto, Hugo Haaring and Hans Scharoun.

The central importance of metamorphosis

Morphology (the science of the form of plants and animals) is an aspect that Steiner saw as central to his intentions as a designer, and was also of interest to other contemporaries. As well as Sullivan and, interestingly, Le Corbusier's teacher Charles L'Eplattenier among others, there was the English scientist D'Arcy Wentworth Thompson whose book *On Growth and Form* was first published in 1917. Steiner's main inspiration, however,

8 Architecture

The Berlin Philharmonia concert hall by Hans Scharoun, 1956–63. 'Can it be an accident that wherever improvised music is heard people tend to gather around the performers in a circle. The psychological basis for this natural process seems self-evident to all; it had only to be transposed into a concert hall.'[5]

was derived from Goethe's scientific work, specifically his discovery of the metamorphic process of development in plant growth and, subsequently, in a number of other natural phenomena which take place in time. In fact it became clear to Goethe that metamorphic change underlies *all* processes of development in the natural world. Steiner later extended the field by means of 'spiritual-scientific' research and found that human and indeed cosmic evolution is based on metamorphosis.[6]

For Goethe, metamorphosis became the key to understanding the transformation of the amorphous undifferentiated substance of the seed into a plant form with its stages of shooting, leafing, flowering, fruiting, and finally seeding again.

By introducing the principle of metamorphic transformation into architectural form, Steiner was doing two things which had not been attempted before. Firstly he was introducing an essentially *time-based* phenomenon to a *spatial* art. Secondly, in doing so, he was giving artistic expression to what he saw as the underlying laws of Creation. This may sound ambitious, at the very least, and Steiner was very conscious of the magnitude of the task he was undertaking. He felt, however, that a beginning should be made. To understand his reasons for doing so we need to look at Steiner's view of the nature and task of architecture in the context of human evolution, and our present stage of human development.

Rudolf Steiner's cosmology — metamorphosis on a macrocosmic scale

In Steiner's cosmology the entire development of the world progresses through a series of great metamorphoses or transformations. It is characteristic of metamorphosis that form appears, disappears and reappears, and that what happens *between* one form and its reappearance in a transformed state is as significant as what manifests *in* each form. Thus the process has a rhythmic, musical quality like the notes in a scale and the intervals between them.

Altogether, Steiner identified seven 'planetary conditions' of Earth evolution, of which our present 'Earth condition' is the fourth and central stage.[7] This seven-stage process follows an inherent lawfulness and is an archetypal metamorphic pattern of change and development, in which an initial form develops by stages to a point of complexity, and then becomes progressively simplified until, finally, a new and higher manifestation of the form is attained.

The spiritual origins of the human body and architecture

Steiner described architecture as arising '...when we project the specific organization of the human body into the space outside it...'[8] By 'specific organization' he was referring to the underlying spiritual organization of the body, laid down in the Old Saturn stage of our evolution (see note 7). As he put it, 'Architecture would never have come into being if man did not now carry within himself the laws which were imprinted on his physical body during the Old Saturn period.' This is one of the enigmas of architecture—that the most material of the arts has its origin in the earliest stage of evolution whose origins, according to Steiner, began in a spiritual environment long before matter existed.

Those who practise, or contemplate, architecture know that it is primarily concerned with the proportions of its elements and the quality of the spaces they enclose. These are, fundamentally, non-material in character. Goethe, for example, called architecture 'frozen music'.

In its primal stage of development then, the human body was a kind of non-material form composed of forces which only later became filled out and 'embodied' in matter. The purest aspect of this materialized form of the body which we have today is the skeleton, the equivalent of the structure which underlies any architectural work. Steiner referred to this aspect of the human body as the '*physical* body' to distinguish it from the aspects of the human being which developed in subsequent evolutionary stages.

The life body and metamorphosis

In the second stage of planetary evolution, called 'Old Sun', the human 'life body' or 'etheric body' had its beginnings. This life body is essentially a rhythmic system of forces which animates and maintains the physical body. Without it, the body would be an inanimate corpse. Steiner refers to the etheric body as the 'architect of the physical body', exerting a formative influence on it. The etheric body is part of the 'etheric world', which is characterized by time processes—of which metamorphosis is the most typical.[9] In making metamorphosis the basis for a new approach to architectural form Steiner was therefore giving expression in physical architectural space to the etheric world's formative time processes. He was, in a sense, raising the dead matter of architecture into the sphere of life. His reason for doing so becomes apparent if we follow the story further.

The origins of consciousness

During the third stage of planetary evolution, known as 'Old Moon', the beginnings of human soul life and emotion arose (or, in spiritual-scientific terminology, the 'astral body') as the basis for consciousness. With our soul/astral body we respond to all outer experiences and make them part of our inner/emotional life. This includes impressions made by art and architecture. In chapter 2 Steiner discusses the effect of architectural forms on us, which are initially absorbed by the soul and then work right down into the physical body. Chapter 4 contains a lecture discussing how the soul's unconscious affinity with geometry enables the spiritual world to 'speak' to us through the underlying geometry of architectural forms.

The self-conscious ego and physical matter

By the beginning of our present stage of evolution, the human being had thus developed a physical body, a 'life

Introduction 13

body' and an 'astral body' during the Old Saturn, Old Sun and Old Moon stages of evolution. A fourth member of our being, the 'I' or 'ego', is being incorporated during this current evolutionary phase, known as 'Earth'. This 'I' is the spiritual core unique to each human being. It is the youngest and least developed aspect of the human being but, to the extent that we can gain access to it, the 'I' enables us to take charge of our own destiny.

The human being's role in future stages of evolution

During our present 'Earth' stage of evolution, the spiritual substance of previous stages has condensed into physical matter. The development of matter at the same time as the development of the human 'I' produces a new situation in evolution. The spatial separation between human beings and their environment, arising through the fact that we now 'inhabit' material bodies, creates a basis for objectivity and freely determining—to some extent—how much, and in what way, we interact with the world. At the same time, this condensing process has the effect of obscuring spiritual forces which underlie the world as we experience it with our normal, physical senses.

Having created the fourfold human being in this way, the spiritual world has withdrawn from our field of vision, thus leaving us free to take responsibility for ourselves and play an essential part in the future course of our cosmic evolution. This future involves further transformation of the human being and our world over the course of the three 'planetary conditions' to come.[10]

Today we face the challenge of seeing through the apparently material nature of the physical body to its underlying spiritual form which originated in Old Saturn, to which it will ultimately return at the end of planetary evolution, at a transformed level.[11]

The future task of architecture

As Steiner saw it, architecture has a central part to play in this process of spiritualization because its laws are also those of the physical body. The great mystery behind both is that these laws are, ultimately, non-material. This is true, even of the laws of levity and gravity (see chapter 1). All architecture worthy of the name makes these laws visible in artistic form, through its proportions and the expression given to its load-bearing elements. The new architecture, Steiner argued, needs to include a further element by expressing the laws of metamorphosis visibly in space. By doing so, he believed, human beings will be able to experience at first hand the underlying spiritual processes through which the human body and the universe were formed. We can then begin to live with these processes so that they become living faculties and capacities, through which we and potentially the world can be transformed.

The reality of reincarnation

The long-term project of transforming the world depends on a continuity of *individual* human consciousness. Otherwise, the notion of a self-determining free human spirit, or 'ego', is not a reality. In Steiner's view, therefore, each individual human spirit returns to earth to renew the task of serving its needs and furthering the course of evolution. Thus all previous and future stages of evolution are accompanied by the evolution and development of each human being. Just as the earth is evolving through a process of metamorphosis, so is each one of us too. Every human life is a metamorphic development of the last life, and during the interval between lives we digest our previous one and prepare our tasks and challenges for the next. To Steiner, therefore, reincarnation is a reality that underpins his entire work. For example, in chapter 2 we find a discussion of the influence of architectural forms on the form of the human body over 'millennia', for which reincarnation is the underlying principle.

Principles of transformation in science and art

There are two themes recurring in Steiner's work that are strongly represented in his discourses on architecture. One, derived originally from Goethe, is that art and science are different representations of the same truths. Thus the theme of metamorphosis, for example, can be observed in nature but can also be represented artistically. This point is taken up in the introduction to chapter 5 and is the background to chapter 6.

The second theme is that art has its own lawfulness which is *different* from the laws and methods of science. Time and again Steiner emphasized, for example, that the forms he incorporated into his first Goetheanum building arose from purely artistic imagination. They were not translations of concepts into symbols, as might be thought from a first encounter with them.

Furthermore, the transforming power of art became central to Steiner's whole endeavour of stimulating people to take responsibility for their own destiny and working towards creating a new world order. As he might have said: science can understand the world, but only art can create a *new* world.

PART ONE

1. The Origins and Nature of Architecture

It is a most remarkable fact that architecture in its highest forms does not bear the least resemblance to anything in nature, that it is peculiarly and exclusively a human work; and yet, long before man came to need it, long before the foundation of the world, at the very beginning, in the councils of eternity, the laws which regulate the art were formed.

Alexander 'Greek' Thomson (1817–75)

The following extracts are taken from a lecture series given in 1914. In the first, Steiner gives a picture of the relationship between the laws of architecture and the nature of 'Old Saturn', during which both the universe and the human physical body had their origins and from which architecture derives its essential nature.

The second extract is concerned with the supersensible forces at work in the physical body, without which we literally could not lift a finger. As Steiner describes it, architecture arises when these forces are projected into space. In this connection he refers to two kinds of forces. One is '...a spatial system of lines and forces ... which forms our physical body through the activity of our etheric body'. The other is the interaction of weight and support, discussed in the third extract. This is both a sensible and a supersensible phenomenon and Steiner presents a kind of architectural meditation in which he invites us to experience the forces of gravity, levity and balance inwardly and, in doing so, to become conscious of the spiritual beings who underlie them.

Taking these passages together we find a profound expression of architecture's potential to become spiritual experience. If, through architecture, forces which exist and work within us are reflected back to us from surrounding space, so that our inner world becomes, in a sense, our outer environment – as Steiner tells us also happens in our life after death – then the effect of architecture on our inner life can be that '... our soul is now no longer only within our body's skin but belongs to the cosmos'.

The cosmic origins of architecture

Architecture would never have come into being if human beings did not now carry within themselves the laws imprinted on their physical bodies during the Old Saturn period. The human being mysteriously projects into the laws of architecture all that he took into his being during the ancient Saturn period. Obviously we have to use such means as are at our disposal today. But the essential and living elements in our architectural activities stem from what was implanted in us during Old Saturn evolution.

Let us enter still deeper into the matter, which we thus place before our souls. What does the human being do when he becomes totally absorbed in the creativity of architecture, either as architect or as the observer or admirer of architecture? He lives within the Saturn laws of

The Origins and Nature of Architecture 21

his physical body. When he immerses himself entirely in the laws of architecture, he becomes once more a 'Saturn' being. All the impressions produced by architecture, its austerity, its chaste proportions, its silence which is yet so eloquent, result from the fact that we immerse ourselves in what was given us by the spirits of the higher hierarchies[1] who were active at the beginning of the Saturn period.

So when human beings create or enjoy architecture (I mean, of course, when this is practised as a true art), they really lift themselves not only out of present earthly existence but also out of the more distant past, placing themselves back once more into the phase of Saturn evolution.[2]

Forces at work in the body...

In our ego we can only contain the *thought* of lifting a hand; this thought must at once act upon the astral body, and the astral body transfers its activity, which lives in it as an impulse, to the etheric body.[3] And what happens then? Let us assume that someone is holding his hand in a horizontal position. Now he forms the idea: I want to raise my hand a little bit higher. The idea, which in life is followed by the act of lifting the hand, passes over to the astral body; there an impulse arises and passes over from the astral body to the etheric body. And now the following happens in the etheric body: the hand is at first horizontal; then the etheric body is drawn up higher, and then the physical hand moves, following what occurs first as a development of force in the etheric body. The physical hand thus follows the etheric.

In the life of our organism we are continually dealing with a development of force followed by a state of equilibrium. Of course the human being has no conscious knowledge of what is really going on within him, but what takes place is so infinitely wise that the cleverness of the human ego is nothing by comparison. We would be unable to move a hand if we had to depend on our own cleverness and knowledge alone, for the subtle forces developed by the astral body in the etheric body and then passed on to the physical body are quite inaccessible to ordinary human knowledge. And the wisdom developed in this process is millions of times greater than that required by a watchmaker in making a watch.

We do not usually think of this, but this wisdom actually has to be developed. The moment the 'I' sends the impulses of its idea into the astral body we need the help of another being, one belonging to the hierarchy of the angels. For even the tiniest movement of a finger we need the assistance of such a being, whose wisdom is far in advance of our own. We could do nothing but lie on the earth immobile, making concepts in utter rigidity, if the beings of the higher hierarchies did not constantly surround us with their activity. Therefore the first step towards initiation is to gain an understanding of how these forces act upon the human being.

...and projected into architecture

I have tried to show here what is involved even in a movement as simple as resting the head in the hand. If we carry this spatial system of lines and forces, which is constantly active in us, out into the world, and if we organize matter according to this system, then architecture arises. All architecture consists in separating from ourselves this system of forces and placing it outside us in space. Thus we may say: Here we have the outer boundary of our physical body, and if we push the inner organization, which has been impressed by the etheric body on to the physical body, outside this boundary, then architecture arises. All the laws present in the architectural utilization of matter are also to be found in the human body. When we project the specific organization of the human body into the space outside it, then we have architecture.

Now we know, in our way of looking at things, that the etheric body is attached to the physical body. Looking once more at any work of architecture, what can we say about it? We can say that here, carried into the space exterior to us, is the interaction between vertical and horizontal and between forces that react together, all of which are otherwise to be found within the human physical body.[4]

Basic elements of architecture, body, soul and cosmos

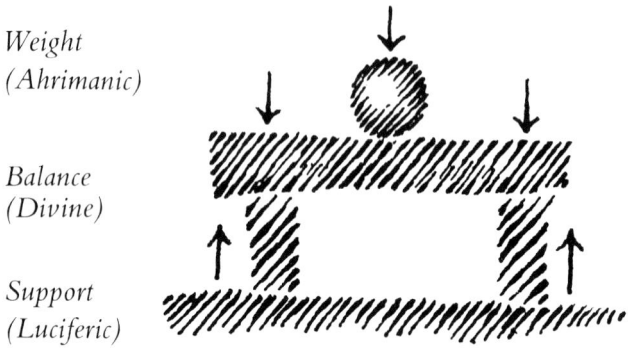

Weight (Ahrimanic)

Balance (Divine)

Support (Luciferic)

We shall gain a lot if, for instance, as well as just seeing this diagram, we try and immerse ourselves in it and try to feel what is going on: weight pressing down here, and weight being supported there.

Let us go even further and not just *look* at it, but *feel* that the beam needs to have a certain strength, otherwise the load will crush it, and the supporting pillars must also have a certain strength, otherwise they too will be crushed. We must feel the way the sphere on top is pressing down, the pillars supporting and the beam keeping the balance. Not until we get right inside the elements of weight, support and balance, between what presses down and what supports, shall we feel our way into the elements of architecture.

The Origins and Nature of Architecture 25

Temple of Aphaia, Aegina

But if we follow a structure of this kind not only with our eye but, as it were, crawl into it and experience the weighing down, the supporting and the balance, then we shall feel that our whole organism is becoming involved, and as if we have to call on an invisible brain belonging to our whole being and not just our head. Then we can awaken to the awareness, 'Ah! Now we are beginning to feel!' To take our simple example, we shall feel a supporting element, an upward striving luciferic element, a weighing and pressing down ahrimanic element, and a balance between the luciferic and ahrimanic which is a divine quality.[5] Thus, even lifeless nature becomes filled with Lucifer and Ahriman and their superior ruler, who eternally brings about the balance between them. If we thus learn to experience the luciferic, ahrimanic and divine elements in architecture, so that architecture affects us inwardly, we shall become conscious of a richer feeling of the world which leads or, one could almost say, pulls the soul into the things of the world. For our soul is now not only within our body's skin but belongs to the cosmos. This is a way of becoming conscious of this.

Architecture producing musical mood

We shall become aware too, that whereas the architectural element, outside us, is supporting, weighing down and creating a balance, we ourselves in this encounter with the architectural element develop a musical mood. Architecture produces a musical mood in our inner being, and we notice that even though the elements of architecture and music appear to be so alien in the outer world, through this musical mood engendered in us, our experience of architecture brings about a reconciliation, a balance between these two elements.[6]

2. The Formative Influence of Architecture on the Human Being

In the following passage Steiner discusses the way that architectural forms influence human beings, initially as a visual experience imprinted subconsciously on the soul and thence, over time, influencing the form of the body. He gives as examples the influence of Gothic cathedrals on the countenances of medieval mystics and the time in the Atlantean age, represented by the biblical story of Noah's Ark, when the human body received the form and proportions it has today.

Yesterday we ended with Noah's Ark, stating that the proportions of its height, breadth and length expressed the proportions of the human body. Now, in order to understand the meaning of this Ark mentioned in the Bible (1 Moses 6:15), we must deepen our knowledge of various things. We must at first make clear to ourselves what it means that a vessel through which man should be rescued has definite dimensions. It will then be necessary to occupy ourselves with that time of man's development in which the actual happenings to which the Noah story refers took place.

The Formative Influence of Architecture 29

The experience of Gothic

When people who understood something of occultism[1] produced some object in the outer world, a quite definite purpose for the soul was always connected with it. Recall the Gothic churches, those characteristic buildings that arose at the beginning of the Middle Ages and spread from Western to Middle Europe. These churches have a definite architectural style, which expresses itself in the arch that consists of two parts joining in a point above. This architectural form permeates the whole as atmosphere—that peculiar arching consisting of two parts tapering up to a point, the whole reaching upward, the columns with a definite form, etc. It would be quite wrong to assert that such a Gothic cathedral was simply a product of outer needs, out of a certain longing perhaps, to create a house of God that should express or mean this or that. Something much deeper underlay this. Those who indicated the first ideas for these Gothic buildings were adepts in occultism. They were, to a certain degree, initiates. It was their purpose to see that whoever entered such a house of God was to receive quite definite soul impressions. When one sees these peculiar archings, when one views the inner space in which the columns rise like trees in a grove, such a House of God works upon the soul quite differently than does a building in which columns support a Roman or Renaissance cupola. Of course, man does not become conscious of the fact that such forms produce

30   Architecture

quite definite effects; they occur in the unconscious. He cannot be rationally clear about what is happening in his soul.

The Church of the Holy Cross in Schwäbisch-Gmünd, Germany

The Formative Influence of Architecture

Ensouled forms and materialistic forms

Many people believe that the materialism of our modern times arises because people read so many materialistic texts. The occultist, however, knows that this is only one of the lesser influences. What the eye sees is of far greater importance, for it has an influence on soul processes that more or less run their course in the unconscious. This is of eminently practical importance, and when spiritual science one day really takes hold of the soul, then its practical effect will become noticeable in public life too. I have often called attention to the fact that walking through the streets in the Middle Ages was a different experience from nowadays. Right and left there were house facades that were built out of what the soul felt and thought. Every key, every lock, carried the imprint of the person who had made it. Try to realize how the individual craftsman felt joy in each piece, how he worked his own soul into it. In every object there was a piece of soul, and when a person moved among such things, soul forces streamed across to him.

Forms experienced in the modern city

Now compare this with a city today. Here is a shoe store, a hardware store, a butcher's shop, then a pub, etc. All this is alien to inner soul processes; it is related only to our outer being, and thus generates soul forces that tend towards materialism. These influences work much more strongly than do the dogmas of materialism. Add to these our horrible art of advertising. Old and young wander through a sea of such abominable products that awaken the most evil forces of the soul. So likewise do our modern comic journals. This is not meant to be a fanatical agitation against these things, but only a description of facts. All this pours a stream of forces into the human soul producing the cultural influences that lead people in a certain direction. The spiritual scientist knows how much depends upon the world of forms in which a human being lives.

The influence of Gothic cathedrals on the Christian mystics

Towards the middle of the Middle Ages there arose along the Rhine that remarkable religious movement called Christian mysticism. It is linked with such leading spirits as Master Eckhart, Tauler, Suso, Ruysbroek, and others. This was a tremendous deepening and intensification of human feeling life because these preachers did not stand alone but had a faithful audience at that time... Because there emanated such a deepening from these great souls, the Rhine was named at that time 'Europe's Great Parson Street'. Do you know where these soul forces were bred that were searching for an inner union with divine forces? They were developed in

The Formative Influence of Architecture   33

the Gothic cathedrals with their pointed arches, pillars and columns. This had educated these souls. What the human being sees, what is poured into his environment becomes a force in him. In accordance with it, he forms himself.

Let us put this before our souls schematically, set against the background of human development and evolution. At a given time an architectural style is born out of the great ideas of initiates. Human souls take up the force of these forms. Centuries go by. What the soul has absorbed through its contemplation of building forms appears in the mood of his soul. Ardent souls will then come into existence, souls who look up to the heights. Even when the course was not always quite as I have described it, similar effects showed themselves often in human development.

Now let us follow these people some millennia further. Those who absorbed the forces of the forms of these buildings into their souls show the expression of their inner soul configurations in their countenances.[2] The entire human shape forms itself through such impressions. What was built thousands of years ago appears to us in human countenances thousands of years later. Thus one recognizes why such arts were practised. Initiates look ahead, into the far future, and see how human beings are meant to become. Hence it is that at a definite time they develop external building forms, on a large scale. By this means the germ of future human epochs is laid.

The environment of Atlantis

When you rightly keep all this in mind, you will understand what occurred at the end of the Atlantean epoch.[3] Air did not exist as it does today; the distribution of air and water was quite different from what it is today. Masses of mist surrounded Atlantis. When you picture to yourself how mist rises, how clouds form, and rain falls, then you have in miniature what happened over enormous expanses of Atlantis during millennia. With the change in outer living conditions human beings also changed. Formerly, a country covered with thick mist masses had people living in it who had a kind of clairvoyance. Gradually rainstorms came; gradually people accustomed themselves to an entirely new way of life, to a new perception, a new awareness. Human bodies had to change. You would be amazed if you were to see pictures of the first Atlantean people. How different they were from people today! Do not believe, however, that this change occurred by itself. Through long periods of time the human souls had to work on these human bodies and bring about effects such as were described by the simple example given of the effects of architectural forms on the feeling life of the soul, which later appeared in their countenances.

Changes to human souls and bodies in Atlantis

How was it when the Atlantean epoch passed over into the post-Atlantean epoch? At first the human soul

The Formative Influence of Architecture 35

underwent change and, in accordance with this, the body subsequently shaped itself. Let us go into this more deeply! Let us picture an old Atlantean. He still had clairvoyant consciousness and this was connected with the environment in which he lived, with the mist-filled atmosphere where he dwelt. Because of this atmosphere, things did not show themselves to him with firmly marked contours. Actually his perceptions were floods of surging, interweaving colours and images. Into this, outlines gradually appeared. Objects revealed themselves like lanterns in the mist, encircled by rainbow colours, and his spiritual capacities developed accordingly. Had this condition continued, it would have been impossible for human beings to acquire the form of body they have today. Objects had to take on their present contours, the air become free of water. This process went on for thousands of years.

The formative task of Noah's Ark

Only gradually did things take on distinctness for human perception. The human soul had to receive new impressions and form its body correspondingly, for in accordance with what you think and feel is your body formed. What kind of form did the soul experience when it emerged from the Atlantean watery landscape into the new airy landscape?

For our present body to shape itself, the human being

had to be surrounded by a form of definite length, breadth and depth. As a matter of fact, this form was given to the human being so that the body could form itself thereby. Just as the mood of the mystics arose out of the shape of the cathedral, with human countenances later shaping themselves accordingly, so did human beings gradually transform themselves as a result of living in vessels which had been built according to particular measurements, under the influence of great initiates.

Before the time of our present humanity there was a kind of water or sea-life lived in vessels, in which humanity gradually accustomed itself to life on land. Life at the end of Atlantis was for the most part a life in ships or vessels. Not only were they surrounded by a watery, misty air, but a large part of Atlantis was covered by the sea. This is the deep mystery of Noah's Ark. What is to be found in the original religious documents has an immense depth. We find radiance of wisdom and sublimity in these ancient records when we immerse ourselves deeply in them.[4]

3. The History of Architecture in the Light of Mankind's Spiritual Evolution

In the passage quoted in chapter 2 Steiner illustrated the effect of architectural forms by examples from history – albeit a very remote period of history in the case of 'Noah's Ark'. In the following passages Steiner discusses the relationship between architectural styles and humanity's more recent spiritual development from the Egyptian period to the present time. The chapter ends by making a connection between Egyptian mummification and the materialistic fixation on the body which is a central aspect of modern culture. This is not an idle speculation on Steiner's part. It is related to his overall conception of evolution which views the 'Graeco-Roman cultural epoch'[1] as the turning-point in the entire process, with 'the Mystery of Golgotha' as its central event. Before that event human beings were on a descending path from their spiritual origins. Following it, we have the potential to tread an ascending path and reconnect with the spiritual world.

The Egyptian period, which came immediately before the 'turning-point' in Graeco-Roman times, played a crucial role in the descending path of human development by connecting mankind's consciousness more firmly to the earth and thereby laying foundations for the later development of self-consciousness and individual freedom (see Introduction). Our present age, commencing with the Renaissance, follows the central Graeco-

Roman time and therefore mirrors the Egyptian period. The danger we face in our own time is of failing to break through the separation, which Egyptian initiates helped to bring about, between our everyday consciousness and our eternal spiritual essence.

Christ's deed on Golgotha gave us the potential to reconnect with our spiritual origins, though now in a more conscious way, provided we can overcome the 'maya' or illusion of materialism. In chapter 4 we shall see how Steiner saw the potential role that architecture can play in making this breakthrough.

The Egyptian pyramid

Let us describe what the Egyptian perceived. He said, 'I see here a corpse, the dust of a human being who was the bearer of an ego; I know—for I know it from ancient tradition and from the experience of my ancestors—that there is something else, a spiritual part, which passes into other worlds. This could not fulfil its task were it to live solely in that spiritual world. A connecting link must be formed between this spiritual part and the earthly world; we must form a magnetic link for the soul which passes at death into higher realms, in order to arouse in it a feeling of permanence, so that it may return again, and appear once more on this earth.'

We know from the teachings of spiritual science that humanity itself takes care that the soul shall return again and again to new incarnations; we know that when a

Architecture in Light of Mankind's Spiritual Evolution 39

Aerial view of Mycerinus' Pyramid

human being passes at death into other spheres, during the period in Kamaloca (that period during which the human being weans himself from what is earthly), he is still chained by certain forces to what is physical. We know that it is these forces which do not allow him to rise at once into the higher spiritual regions of Devachan, and that it is they also which draw the human being down again to a new incarnation. But we are a people today who live in abstractions, and who represent such things as theories. In ancient Egypt all this lived as tradition. The Egyptian was the reverse of a theorist or mere thinker. He wanted to perceive with his senses how the soul took its way from the dead body into higher realms—he wanted to have this constructed before him. These thoughts he embodied in the pyramids: the way the soul rises, how it leaves the body, how it is still partly fettered, and how it is led upwards to higher regions. In the architecture of the pyramids we can see the fettering of the soul to what is earthly; we can see how Kamaloca with its mysterious forms appears before us; and we can say that it is an outer symbol of the soul which has left the body and is rising into higher realms.

The Greek temple

Let us now pass from the Egyptian pyramid to the Greek temple. This temple will only be understood by those who are able to inwardly grasp and feel the forces at work in space. The Greek possessed this feeling. Anyone studying space from the standpoint of spiritual science knows that it is not the absolute void of which our ordinary mathematicians and physicists dream, but that it is differentiated. It is something that is filled with lines, with lines of force in this direction and in that, from above downwards, from right to left, straight and curved lines going in every direction. Space may be felt, it may be penetrated with feeling... When art still possessed occult traditions, these mutually supporting forces that existed in space, that streamed hither and thither, were acknowledged. They were perceived by those in whose minds the thought

Architecture in Light of Mankind's Spiritual Evolution   41

Temple at Segesta, Greece

of the Greek temple originated. They did not think out these forms, but they perceived forces streaming through space—and filled them with stone; what was already apparent to supersensible perception they filled with substance. Hence the Greek temple is a material presentation of actual forces working in space; a Greek temple is a crystallized spatial idea in the purest sense of the word. This led to something very important. By giving material expression to force-forms in space, the Greeks gave divine spiritual beings the opportunity of using these material forms. It is no figure of speech but a fact when we say that gods came down at that time into the Greek temples in order to be among human beings on the physical plane.

Just as today parents make available a physical form, the body of flesh, to the child, so that spirit can express itself on the physical plane, so something similar took place in the case of the Greek temple. The opportunity was provided for divine spiritual beings to stream down and incarnate in architectural structure. That is the secret of the Greek temple. The god was present in the temple. Those who felt the form of the Greek temple aright felt that there need be no human being anywhere near it, nor in the temple itself; and yet it would not be empty, for the god was really present there. The Greek temple is a whole, it is complete in itself, because it has the forms which magically draw the god into it.[2]

This dwelling place of the god is inconceivable without the Greek landscape surrounding it, just as later Roman temples are inconceivable without the surrounding countryside. They belong together. I have already pointed out that a Greek temple is complete in itself

Architecture in Light of Mankind's Spiritual Evolution 43

even when there are no people inside it, for its whole conception is that of the dwelling place of the god, whose statue may stand within. People are all around in the countryside. No one enters the temple, yet it stands there, complete in itself — a dwelling place of the god. In every detail we see how people expressed in the decorative forms of these dwelling places of the gods all that their feelings of veneration made them believe they ought to do for the gods. You will recall that in my last lecture I attempted to show you that the motif on the capitals has its origin in the motif of a dance that was performed as homage to the gods of nature. Thus, in the Greek capital, first in painting and then in relief, people applied to the dwelling place of the god what they themselves imagined and felt to be for the glory and veneration of the gods.

The Christian church and the Greek temple compared

Let us now pass on to the forms of earliest Christian architecture. One thought in particular must arise when we pass from the Greek temple to the Christian church.

The Greek temple stands within its surrounding territory; it belongs to its environment. The people are not inside the temple but live around it. The temple belongs to the countryside and is thought of as the sacred place of the countryside. It hallows everything, even the most ordinary daily occupations of the people who live round about. Service rendered to the earth becomes a service rendered to the gods because the god stands or sits in his dwelling place as the ruler. The god participates in work on the land and in the pursuits of the people living around the temple. People feel united with the god as they work on the surrounding land. Worship of the god is not yet separate from service to the earth. The temple grows out of the human element, sometimes indeed out of the all-too-human element, participating in all the good and not-so-good things that go on all around it. 'Earth—be firm, reliable and support us!' is the prevailing mood during the fourth post-Atlantean epoch, when human beings are still one with the earth which the gods have given into their charge, when the human ego is still slumbering in a kind of dream consciousness, when human beings still feel connected with the group soul of the whole of humanity. Then gradually they grow away from this group soul, becoming more and more individual. They separate the worship they perform in their spiritual life from the land, from daily life and activity.

In the early days of Christianity people's feelings were no longer the same as in the Greek age. We see the Greek sowing his fields and working at his trade, pervaded by the unshakable feeling that: 'The temple stands there and the god is within, while I am nearby; I may follow my trade and work on the land, and all the while the god is dwelling there within the temple.'

Architecture in Light of Mankind's Spiritual Evolution 45

The early Christian and Romanesque church

But then the human being became more of an individual; a stronger sense of ego arose within him. Something that had been prepared through the course of long ages by the ancient Hebrew civilization now emerged, particularly in Christianity. Out of the human soul there arose the need to *separate off from the affairs of everyday life* the worship offered to the god. The sacred building was separated from its surrounding territory, and the Christian church came into being. The territory became independent, and within it the building became independent, a territory in itself.

Whereas the Greek temple was an altar for the whole surrounding countryside, the walls of the Christian church now excluded these very surroundings. An interior space was set apart for those who worship. The forms of Christian churches, including those of Romanesque architecture, gradually came to express this individual, spiritual need of the human being, and we can only understand these buildings when we view them from this point of view.

Because of the way the individual Greek lived in his body on the earth he said: 'I can remain here with my flocks, plying my trade and doing my work on the land, for the temple stands over there like an altar for the whole countryside; and within it dwells the god.' Then through Christianity a different feeling arose in the human being and he said: 'I must leave my work and

Durham Cathedral, England, 1110–33

Architecture in Light of Mankind's Spiritual Evolution

trade to worship, for the god has to be sought in there, inside the church.' Earthly worship and heavenly worship became separated.

Architecture gradually adapted to the human being's need for individuality and thus Christian churches increasingly took on a form that would have been quite unsuitable for Graeco-Roman times. This is a form which reveals that the congregation belongs inside it; and gradually separated from the congregation was the part set aside for the priests and the teachers. An enclosed world arose within a world that had itself already been enclosed within walls. Here the spirit spoke to those who sought the spirit. The feeling of the Greeks and Romans for the whole world was the same as that felt by the Christians for the space within their church. What the Greek temple as a whole had been now became the chancel with the altar. An image of the world was sought in the forms of church architecture, whereas in earlier times people took the world as it was and only added what was not visible to the physical senses, namely, the dwelling place of the god.

The Gothic church

Gothic architecture is, essentially, only a further development of what had been prepared earlier. Its main feature is that the bearing of weight is transferred from walls to pillars.

48   Architecture

Reims Cathedral, France, thirteenth–fifteenth century

What is the origin of this whole mode of construction, where weight rests on the pillars, which are so formed that they are able to bear it? The system of construction of the Greek temple is based on quite a different conception. It is as though the human being had got to know the force of gravity inside the earth; and then, finding

Architecture in Light of Mankind's Spiritual Evolution 49

himself placed on the surface of the earth, he makes use of gravity, and by doing so overcomes it. That is the Greek temple, which is the dwelling place for the god. In the weight-bearing pillars of Gothic architecture, on the other hand, we are no longer concerned with the effects of gravity as such but with the work of the human being. Gothic architecture requires individual craftsmanship. The wish to create an enclosed world for the congregation gives rise in Gothic architecture to the need to create something wherein the activity of the congregation plays a part. What the people in the congregation have learnt is embodied in the forms they create. The art of the craftsmen flows into the Gothic forms, and in studying these forms we see the work of human beings who have all worked together contributing their share in the town community.

In older Romanesque churches the building is intended to enclose the congregation as well as the god. In Gothic churches we have a building built by the congregation to enclose the God and to which the craftsmen have added their contribution.[3] They do not only go to church but as a congregation they also share in building it. In Gothic architecture the labour of human beings unites with the divine. Their souls no longer receive the divine as a matter of course; they gather not only to listen to the word of the spirit proceeding from the altar but also to work together and bring to their God what they have learnt. Gothic churches are really crystallized craftsmanship.[4]

50 ARCHITECTURE

The 'Leaves of Southwell', carvings in the Chapter House at Southwell Minster, Nottinghamshire, England, thirteenth century

Architecture in Light of Mankind's Spiritual Evolution 51

Our own age in relation to the Egyptian age

From this we can see how in time human thought and human perception progresses. Thus we arrive gradually at our own age. And we shall see how the forces of evolution are at work not only on the surface, but that hidden occult currents are active also—so that what is taking place today in our civilization appears as a re-embodiment of much that was sown within humanity in ancient Egyptian times.

What constitutes the materialism of our present civilization? What is the special characteristic of the person who, when he wishes to see something spiritual, has lost the harmony that reconciles faith and knowledge? He sees nothing! He observes the gross, material, physical part of the world; he feels it to be real, that it exists, and he even comes to deny what is spiritual. He believes that man's existence is finished when his corpse lies in the earth; he sees nothing rising up into spiritual worlds. Can a conception such as this be the outcome of something that was sown at a time when there was firm faith in the continued life of the soul, such as existed in Egypt? Yes, for civilization does not simply repeat itself as in the vegetable kingdom, where like springs from like again and again, one seed continually giving rise to a similar plant. In civilization one characteristic gives rise to another, which is apparently dissimilar to it and yet may contain deep, intimate resemblances and relationships.

The vision of the human being is confined today to the

Architecture in Light of Mankind's Spiritual Evolution 53

physical body. One regards this as a reality; one cannot raise oneself to what is spiritual. The souls who now look upon their own physical bodies with their eyes, and are unable to rise to what is spiritual, were incarnated among earlier peoples as Greeks, as Romans, and as ancient Egyptians. All that exists in our souls today is the result of what we acquired in previous incarnations.

Imagine your soul back in its Egyptian body. Imagine your soul after death being led up again by way of the pyramid into higher spheres but your body held fast in mummified form. This fact had an occult consequence. The soul had always to look down upon its mummified body below; its thoughts grew harder, more solidified, through focus on and confinement to the physical world. It was forced to look down from the realms of the spirit upon its embalmed physical body, and in consequence the thought became rooted in it that the physical body had a higher reality than it actually had. Imagine a human being, as soul, looking down at that time upon his mummy. Thought about the physical world hardened; such thought passed through repeated incarnations, and now is such that we cannot extricate our thoughts from physically embodied form.[5]

4. A New Architecture as a Means of Uniting with Spiritual Forces

Materialism, in Steiner's perspective, is an essential stage in human evolution because separation from the spiritual world, which it involves, enables us to become independent of the spiritual beings who created us. In this 'freedom space' we have the potential to reconnect with the spiritual world out of our own latent spiritual faculties. Art and architecture have an essential role to play in this process, by expressing formative spiritual forces in wholly material form.

The following lecture is one of a series given to the co-workers engaged in building the first Goetheanum in Dornach, Switzerland. Steiner begins by comparing the task of the new architecture with that of Greek and Gothic. The task of achieving a 'complete union with the spirit' requires the development of forms which give expression to dynamic creative forces. As he puts it later in the lecture '...the Spirits of Movement stand behind the Spirits of Form'.

There follows an interesting discussion of the qualities of different geometric forms, starting with the relationship between the circle and the 'I' or ego and leading on to the ellipse and the lemniscate (figure of eight). As always with Steiner, this discussion is not entirely academic. As he says, the astral body is a natural geometrician and connects subconsciously with the underlying geometry of architecture. In the case of the first

Goetheanum the geometry is based on two circles that overlap, thereby creating a lemniscate – an inherently dynamic form.

The second half of the lecture relates to the two sets of seven columns that bounded the north and south sides of the first Goetheanum's auditorium – the larger of the two circles. We shall meet other aspects of these in chapter 6 but here Steiner discusses the basic situation of load and support from a point of view that may appear surprising: that of human development as seen from a spiritual perspective.

The building for our time

The point I made before was that another real advance in architectural conception must be achieved in our time, and that this will only be possible if the search for the spirit, which became increasingly apparent from the period of Greek architecture onwards to the Gothic conception, can gradually be transformed into a complete union with the spirit. This means that a building which is now to be dedicated to life inherently linked with the spirit must in its very forms express an intimate correspondence with the spiritual world. By not explaining this in abstraction but grasping it instead with our whole life of feeling and soul, we could say that everything entering into and living in our soul through spiritual science is the very life in the forms we are creating. The spirit is experienced as free, having now descended to mankind.

The Greeks placed the temple into the countryside like an altar. But the future—and also the present, in so far as we are working out of the future in our building—places the spirit itself, and all that it expresses, into the landscape. What the spirit expresses in forms is of course a kind of speaking, something that speaks to human beings today. For this to come about, we must endeavour to comprehend the spirit in the forms it generates. In order to understand the Greek temple, we tried last time to grasp the purely physical qualities of space and of gravity. But the spirit does not only work according to the laws of mechanics and dynamics, nor does it reveal itself solely in terms of space and the forces active in structure. The spirit lives, and hence it must be expressed in our building in a living way, a truly living way. We shall not understand this any better if we begin to interpret the spirit symbolically. The only way is to feel that the forms are alive, that they are organs for what is spoken by the spiritual world.

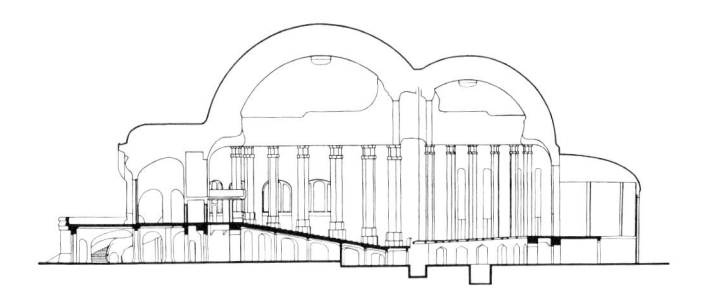

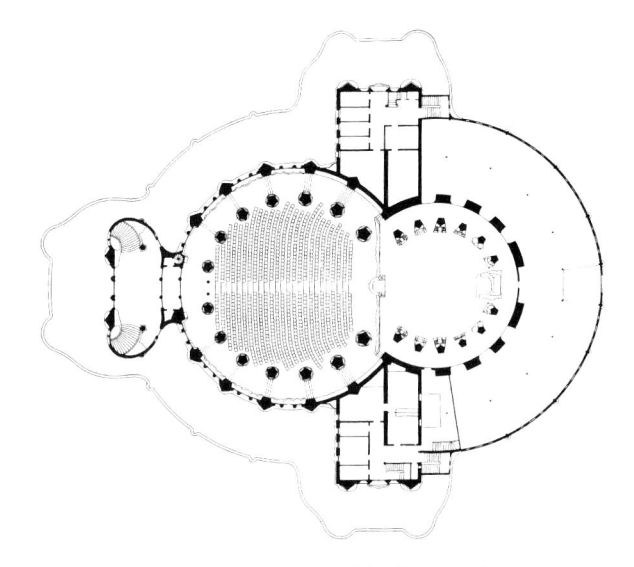

New Architecture Uniting with Spiritual Forces

Ground plan and section of the first Goetheanum

To feel a circle is to feel our 'I'

Can forms speak out of the spiritual world? They can indeed, and they can express many things. Take a concept that is especially close to us, being on the one hand the expression of the highest, while on the other hand, in its luciferic aspect,[1] it is submerged in the lowest. Take the concept of the ego, the concept of the self.

We do not as yet attach anything particularly significant to the expression 'I', or 'self'. Many epochs will have to run their course in human history before a fully conscious mental image can arise in the soul when the word 'I' or 'self' is uttered. But there is a form we can make through which egohood or selfhood can be sensed. When we pass from having a purely mathematical conception of a form to really feeling what a form is, a perfect circle will give us a sense of egohood, of selfhood. To feel a circle means to feel selfhood. To feel a circle in a plane, or a sphere in space, is to feel the self, the ego. Once you have grasped this you will readily follow the rest. When a human being who is truly alive to what he feels is confronted with a circle and in consequence feels a sense of ego, of self, arising in his soul, when even a part of the circle or a fragment of a sphere rouses in him a sense of independence in his own self, then he is learning to live in forms. Those whose feelings are truly alive are good at living in forms. If you bear this in mind you will find it easy to understand what follows from it.

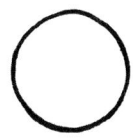

New Architecture Uniting with Spiritual Forces

The first circle I have drawn here has an unbroken line. It can be varied by drawing a wavy line or by making it jagged. In each case it is still a circle, but what do the different forms mean? The second signifies that the self or ego has entered into a relationship with its environment. The simple circle makes us feel that the rest of the world is not there and only what is enclosed within the circle exists. The second circle does not make it seem as though what it encloses is all alone in the world. The wavy line expresses an interaction, an interplay with the environment. Someone who has a living sense for what the forms are saying will feel in regard to the second circle that the inside is stronger than what is outside, whereas in the case of the third circle such a person will feel that the outside is stronger and has forced its way towards the inside.

If we now enter a building and perceive fragments of circles or rounded surfaces with variations of this kind, we shall feel, in the case of jagged surfaces, that what is outside has been stronger, while in the case of undulating surfaces we shall sense that the inside has been the victor. Our soul begins to live with the forms. We do not merely look *at* them, but our soul has the living, surging feeling of victory or encroachment, overcoming or being vanquished. Our soul comes alive and begins to live in the

60 ARCHITECTURE

forms. This union with form, this living in form, is the very essence of true artistic feeling.

The architecture of inner movement

We can go further still, by drawing a more complicated variation. Here the form is moving in a particular direction and becomes action. When we live in this form we have the feeling that it moves and is advancing. The form itself is characteristic of movement.

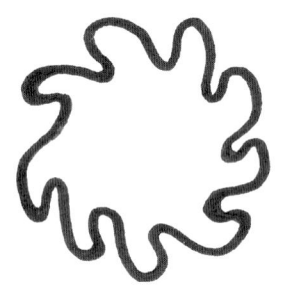

I have here made a simple sketch of something that will appear in a complicated form in our building, and yet you will find that the result is entirely homogeneous. Going from the western entrance through the auditorium towards the stage, you will find that all the forms in the interior evoke the feeling that everything is proceeding from west to east. This is expressed by the forms. Entering the building from the west you will have the idea in your

New Architecture Uniting with Spiritual Forces 61

feelings that you are being borne along in a carriage towards the spiritual east. The very essence and meaning of these variations in the sculptured surfaces is that they do not merely envelop us like dead, dynamic or mechanical forms; we seem to enter a vehicle, a carriage that bears us onwards. In a spiritual sense we shall not be at rest in our building; we shall be led ever onwards.

You will now realize that the fundamental character of the forms here is quite different from that of the forms in the three historical stages of architectural conception I described earlier. Hitherto the concept of architecture has been concerned with the qualities of lifeless, mechanical stasis. Now, however, the concept of architecture becomes a concept of speaking, of moving inwardly, of being drawn along by something. This is one aspect of what is new in our concept of architecture. The basic shape, however, has to correspond to this, and we must now ask how it is achieved.

We have already pointed out that the circle or sphere is the closest to us because it engenders the impression of the self, the ego. This is because a simple sphere or circle is, of all forms, the most easily perceptible. It is an absolutely easy matter to define a circle. All you need is the familiar idea that everything is equidistant from the central point. Picture a whole lot of points at an equal distance from the centre and you have a sphere or a circle. It is the easiest of all thought processes, and thus the circle is the least mysterious of all forms. This also corresponds with external reality, for the self in every living creature, from the simplest cell to the complex human being, gives us the most ordinary, everyday impression, just as a sphere or circle gives us the most ordinary impression.

Behind all this there is, however, something much more profound, and I now want you to follow me in a thought that will lead those who really understand it to great depths.

The ellipse — the curve of addition

An ellipse is a form somewhat more complicated than a circle. Here is the ellipse we are all used to seeing. It need not be exact so long as it is generally recognizable. Passing from the circle to the ellipse we find ourselves with a thought that is no longer quite so simple. Although the ellipse lacks the evenness of the circle, it nevertheless has a regular shape. For politeness sake we will assume that you all know a little geometry, though you may have forgotten some of it. But those who have studied geometry will find it easier to understand the ideas I am about to explain.

An ellipse is a regular form. While the circle relates to a single point, the ellipse relates to two. The line segments between any point of the ellipse and the two foci will naturally differ in length, but the sum of these two lengths will be constant.

You can add the distance of each point from these two foci and you will always get the same length. In the case of the circle this is so simple that there is no need for any

New Architecture Uniting with Spiritual Forces

Ellipse

$a + b = c + d$

Curve of addition

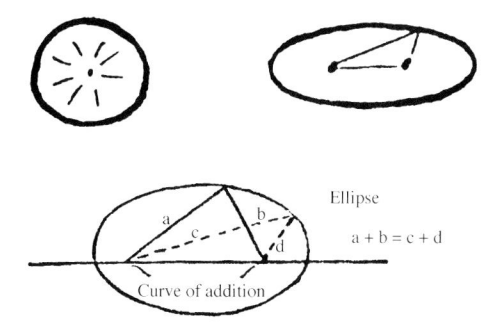

mental process. In the case of the ellipse, however, we must make an addition. All lines to the centre of a circle are equal, but in the ellipse we have to make an addition.

The astral body is a geometrician

You might now wish to point out that you do not, in fact, do any adding up when you see an ellipse. This is true, but your astral body does; what the geometrician does consciously the astral body does unconsciously, for it is a fully trained geometrician. You have no idea of all of the knowledge that is contained in your astral body. In it you are an immensely learned geometrician, only of course the geometry you know in your astral body can only be brought into consciousness with considerable effort. Everything is present down there in your astral body, and if those who teach geometry could instead utilize a pump they would no longer have any need for their usual teaching methods. The knowledge would well up of its own accord. We add, then, the two distances from the foci and always get the same result. What does it really mean when we find beauty in an ellipse? It means that our astral body is adding up and the sum total is always the same. Imagine yourself adding up without knowing it and every time getting the same answer. You feel pleased. From this point you get the same result, and then from that one again, and this fills you with delight. This is the living experience of the ellipse.

In the case of the circle there is no such feeling of delight, for the circle is so immediately obvious. The ellipse causes us greater pleasure because there we have to be inwardly active. The more we are inwardly active, the greater the pleasure we experience. People find it so difficult to realize that the human being, in his inner being, craves for activity. It is only in his conscious life that he wants to be lazy. The astral body is not only wiser, but also more industrious and would like to be active all the time.

The hyperbola — the curve of subtraction

Let us turn to another curve, one that consists of two portions. Those of you who have studied geometry will know that the hyperbola consists of two symmetrical branches. It also has two foci, situated approximately here [*see drawing*]. Again we can draw lines to these two points. The strange thing is that instead of adding we now sub-

New Architecture Uniting with Spiritual Forces 65

tract. We always get the same result by subtracting the lesser from the greater. Our astral body subtracts and is pleased that the difference is always the same. In this inner feeling of two things being equal the astral body experiences how the hyperbola comes into being.

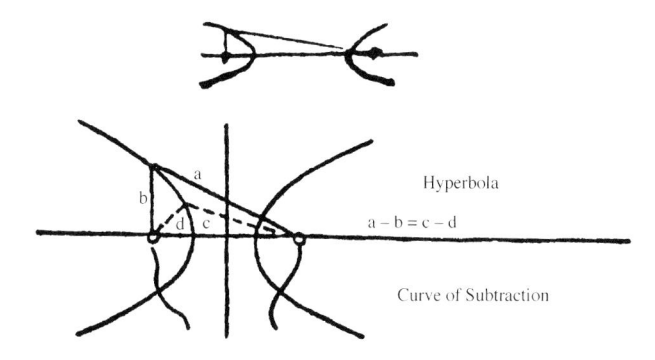

Hyperbola

$a - b = c - d$

Curve of Subtraction

The lemniscate — the curve of multiplication

We are unconscious calculators, and by means of subconscious calculation we create regularity of form. We add and subtract, and we can also multiply. Again we have two points, and by multiplying a by b and c by d we again arrive at a curve that resembles an ellipse although it is not the same. This curve contains an inner process of multiplication and is rather mysterious. A circle is perfectly simple, an ellipse somewhat more complicated and a hyperbola more complicated still, since most people do not realize that it is in fact one curve, although it looks like two. This next curve is mysterious in a different way because, depending on the result of the multiplication, it changes into this curious shape. This multiplication curve, the lemniscate, is the very curve that plays such an important part in occult investigations. It can even go so far as to transform as shown below:

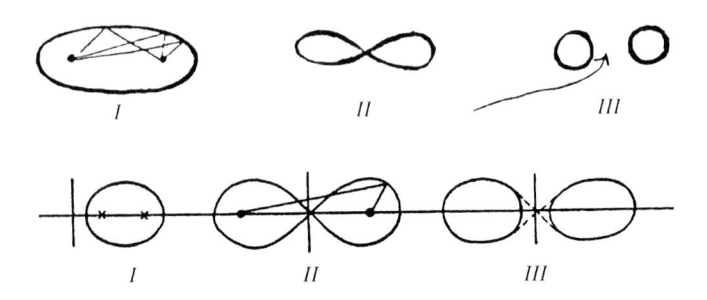

Again this looks like two curves although inwardly they are one, and when our astral body senses that they are one we know that this form [III] is merely a special case of this one [II]. But now imagine that the crossing point disappears together [III] with the curve and then it reappears in the physical world once more. It disappears again and then reappears again. It is one curve that keeps disappearing. You could say that this multiplication curve has three different forms.

The circle — the curve of division

We have so far looked at a curve arising from addition, one arising from subtraction, and another arising from

New Architecture Uniting with Spiritual Forces 67

multiplication. So you might expect there to be a curve arising from division as well. It would be a matter of dividing two distances instead of adding, subtracting or multiplying them. It would have to be possible for our astral body to determine two points and also other points. If it were to divide the longer line segment by the shorter one, and here the longer by the shorter, and so on, a curve would result—which is this circle. All the points are chosen so that their distances from these two points result in the same answer when they are divided. By adding we arrive at the ellipse, by subtracting we arrive at the hyperbola, by multiplying we arrive at the Cassini curve, the lemniscate, and by dividing we arrive at the circle.

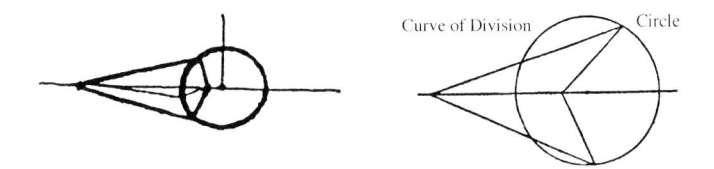

Curve of Division   Circle

We have now come to something very remarkable indeed. When we really try to penetrate them fully, the depths of nature rise up before our soul in all their wonder. A circle at first appears to be an entirely simple matter, and then we discover it to be full of mystery. One way of understanding it is by dividing in relation to two points; a circle comes about when the result is the same in each case. It is quite remarkable, being on the one hand so ordinary that it is easily comprehended, while on the other hand it is the result of hidden division made conscious. It is the same in the case of the human self. The ordinary self is an everyday entity, while the higher self is something mysterious resting in the depths of our soul, a self that can only be found when we transcend its limits and pay heed to the world with which it is connected. The circle is the same whether we say that it is the simplest of all forms or that the product of division from two points is always equal. Within us we have the same duality: something that belongs to everyday life and is readily perceptible and something that we only grasp when we go out into the whole universe, conceiving of this entity as the most complicated product of the great cosmic struggle where Ahriman and Lucifer[2] carry out the division in relation to which our own higher self has to maintain itself as the quotient if it is to come to expression.

Portions of ellipse and of hyperbola, and also of the lemniscate, will be found everywhere in our building, and your astral body will have plenty of opportunity to make these calculations. Mention of one instance will suffice. When people in our building look up to the gallery where the organ and choir will be, their souls will be able to carry out multiplications. Though they may not do so consciously, they will feel it in their depths because the curve of the structure around the organ will call for multiplication. The same curve will be found in many other places as well.

Path from the lower to the higher self

After what I have now told you about the twofold significance of the circle you will be able to realize, when you enter the building from the west and feel yourselves surrounded by the circular structure, and by the dome above, that here is the image of the human self. But the smaller interior to the east will not at first sight be so intelligible. The smaller structure will seem to be full of mystery because, although its form is also circular, it must be conceived of as the result of a process of division, and it only outwardly resembles the larger space. There are two circles, but the one corresponds to everyday life while the other is connected with the whole cosmos. We bear within us a lower self and a higher self, yet both are one. Thus our building had to be a twofold structure. Its form expresses the dual nature of man—not in any symbolic sense but because the form is as it is. When the curtain in front of the stage is open we shall sense an image of the human being not only as he is in everyday life, but as a complete being. Because the forms express a movement from west to east, they directly express the path of the lower to the higher self.

Everything I have been telling you can be felt in the forms. A building of this kind reveals how nature's spiritual forms and also the higher spiritual world can be expressed in a manner befitting both nature and spirit. Those who try to think out all kinds of ingenious interpretations will fail to understand our building, for it can only be comprehended by a living sense of how its forms come into being and of what their essence is. That is why I do not want to describe it in pictures. I want to tell you how it developed and how spirit itself became form and movement and flowed into our building.

Our seven pairs of life pillars

As we appear on earth we are highly complex. When we first arrive we cannot stand upright. We crawl; indeed, at first we cannot even do that. Then gradually we master the forces that allow us to become upright. A diagram will help us to explore what is involved. Here is the earth [*drawing begins – see on page 71*]. First we live in the horizontal; subsequently we stand up and become vertical. We achieve this vertical stance out of our own human nature, but we have the help of all the hierarchies throughout our life. What helps us to stand up and to walk are the forces that rise up from the earth and work towards the expanse of the cosmos. Here [*see drawing*] are these earthly forces. Today physicists speak only of physical forces of attraction and gravity. The earth, however, is not merely a physical body but a being of spirit and soul, and when, as little children, we raise ourselves to the upright position and walk, we are uniting ourselves with the forces of will rising up out of the earth. This earth-will permeates our being; we allow it to flow through us, we place ourselves upright—in the direction

New Architecture Uniting with Spiritual Forces 71

of the earth-will, making it our ally. In opposition to the earth-will, however, there is another will that presses in from all directions of the cosmos. Although we are unaware of it, forces are working in from all sides as we raise ourselves to the upright position. We collide with these forces that are pouring in from outside as we stand up.

Cranium
Man at first horizontal
Will
Earth

This situation no longer has any particular significance here on earth, but during the period of ancient Moon it was immensely significant. Conditions at that time were such that from our earliest childhood we had a different orientation from that of the present time, in that we had to place ourselves within the direction of the moon-will. As a result of this we acquired the first beginnings of our cranium. Nowadays this is something we inherit, but at the time of ancient Moon it was a question of acquiring it. We had to push away the will forces coming from outside—rather as a locomotive pushes away snow—compressing our soft cranium so that it became hard. Today this is something we inherit. We no longer have to create the bones of our skull. But we do still create them in our ether body, for as we rise to the upright position there is a densification in the head resulting from the battle between forces streaming out from the earth and those streaming in from all around.

From this we can go on to say that in observing the ether body we still find that with both legs we set up vertical lines with which we work against the forces coming in from outside. We can then observe the resulting densification that creates this form [*see drawing below*]. We stand. Our physical legs go up as far as our torso, but our etheric legs go up further. Thus the ether body of our head is densified, and so even today our densified etheric head arises through the formation of the brain. This does not only take place in childhood; it continues as we pass through seven periods of life. From the first to the seventh year, from the seventh to the fourteenth, and so on, more and more vertical lines of varied forces come into being. By the time we have become fully mature human beings at the respectable age of 50, we have added pair after pair to those first strong pillars that we built up during our first seven years. They appear in the ether body in different colours. With every pair of what I will call 'life pillars' we

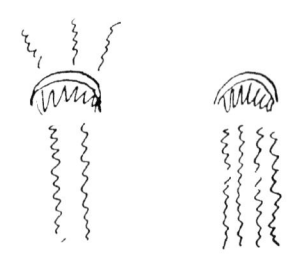

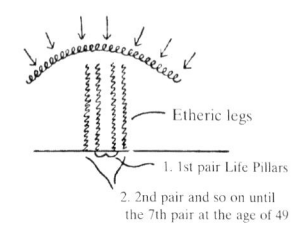

Etheric legs
1. 1st pair Life Pillars
2. 2nd pair and so on until the 7th pair at the age of 49

New Architecture Uniting with Spiritual Forces 73

Rear of the auditorium in the first Goetheanum

strengthen our etheric cranium. At the end of our first seven years the first pair is completed, at 14 the second, at 21 the third, until finally at 49 the seventh pair is there. With every pair of these life pillars we bear our etheric cranium more securely.

Need you do more than imagine the way we human beings go through life raising up within ourselves every seven years differently shaped pairs of pillars that bear our cranium? Surely not! Once you perceived this you will have acquired a living understanding of the inner form of the larger round section of our building. Entering from the west you find that up to the first pair of columns it is like the human being developing during our first seven years, and that up to the second pair it is like the development from our seventh to our fourteenth year, and then to 21, and so on. Around you, you continue to have the cranium. Here, cast into form, is the human being as we really are, as we live in our ether body.

Four steps in earthly evolution: Greek, early Christian, Gothic, and our time

It is in this way that Gothic architecture will be transformed into the architecture of spiritual science. In Gothic times people prayed: 'O Father of the universe, may we be united with you, in your spirit.' Gothic architecture expresses this. Those who can bring themselves to accept what is granted in answer to this prayer, and who truly

New Architecture Uniting with Spiritual Forces

understand the living development of spiritual science, will be able to solve the riddle of human beings and our evolution. As the forms in our architecture endeavour to unite with the spirit—though they express only the endeavour as yet—so we will begin to feel that we have become spiritualized human beings within a building that clearly expresses the inner nature of the human being, comprehending ourselves in our inner living being.

'We dwell in the open countryside, and the spirit is amongst us.' So speaks the idea of Greek architecture.

'While we abide in the sanctuary the spirit comes to us.' So speaks the idea of early Christian architecture.

'We abide in the church, and our soul is uplifted as we raise ourselves in anticipation to the spirit.' So speaks the idea of Gothic architecture.

'We enter with reverence into the spirit in order that we may become one with the spirit that is poured out in forms around us, because the Spirits of Form are around us, and these forms move because the Spirits of Movement stand behind the Spirits of Form.' So speaks the idea of the new architecture!

Thus the modes of existence change through the stages of earthly evolution; and it is the human being's task to understand its inner sense and meaning. We only keep pace with evolution when we endeavour, in every epoch, to experience what the spiritual world bestows in that epoch.

Why do we as souls pass through different, successive incarnations? It is not in order to experience the same things over and over again; not in order to experience the Renaissance and then again the Renaissance, but in order to assimilate into our souls whatever is new in all that the spiritual world pours forth. In this sense we are now at a turning-point in human evolution—in the sphere of art as well as other spheres of cultural life—where the spirit is clearly setting us new riddles. Just as the Renaissance was a time when people strove to find their new direction by referring to what had existed in the past, so we are now in a similar position with regard to our knowledge and perception of the universe. What the modern age has yielded since the sixteenth century has been a preparation for precisely this experience of the universe in its forms and movements that now appear as riddles before us.

This is all for today. In another lecture I will try to approach questions of a still more intimate character, relating to the living soul of nature in connection with colour and painting.[3]

5. Art and Architecture as Manifestations of Spiritual Realities

It is not the external form that is real, but the essence of things. For this truth, it is impossible for someone to express something real by imitating the surface of things.

Constantin Brancusi, 1926

If, as Steiner argued, architectural forms have a direct effect on human beings, then questions of style and form cease to be the subjective issues to which we have become accustomed. It is clear from chapter 4 that when Steiner talks about architecture having the potential to bring about a union between the human being and the spiritual world he is not thinking in terms of a symbolic language. Instead he sees architecture as having the capacity to make supersensible phenomena manifest and visible in space.

This conception of architecture – and, in fact, any of the arts – originates from Goethe's view of art and science as having a common source in the world of archetypes. A phenomenon that takes a supersensible form in the spiritual world can, in the sense world, either take the form of a scientific truth or be manifested through art. Some aspects may be better seen through one 'window' and some through another. Hence Goethe's statement (which Steiner refers to in the following passage): 'Beauty is a manifestation of secret laws of nature that would have remained

78 Architecture

forever hidden had beauty not appeared.' Therefore, far from being subjective, art is another means of experiencing truth. It can, in fact, become a research tool.[1]

In the following passage Steiner discusses architectural motifs as pictorial expressions of essentially supersensible experiences. As he sees it, the craftsman may have drawn on natural forms — in this case plant forms — as a means of expression, but not in the sense of decorative imitation.

The extent to which materialism asserted itself in all spheres of life during the second half of the nineteenth century was enough to drive anyone to despair. I still remember how many sleepless nights the question of the Corinthian capital gave me. The main feature of the Corinthian capital, its principle decoration—although 'decoration' was virtually a forbidden word at the time of which I am speaking—is the acanthus leaf. What could be more obvious than to infer that the acanthus leaf on the Corinthian capital and elsewhere was simply the result of naturalistic imitation of the leaf of the common acanthus plant? A sensitivity for art, however, should make it very difficult to accept that somewhere along the line a beginning was made by taking the leaf of a weed, an acanthus leaf, making a carving of it and sticking it onto a Corinthian capital. Let me draw a rough sketch of the leaf of *Acanthus spinosus,* the ordinary spiny acanthus, which is supposed to have been carved in stone and then added to the Corinthian capital:

Manifestations of Spiritual Realities   79

Acanthus leaf by Rudolf Steiner from his notebook, June 1914

Vitruvius on the origins of the Corinthian capital

Here we have to remember Vitruvius, the scholarly cataloguer of the artistic traditions of antiquity. He quotes a well-known anecdote that led to the adoption of the 'basket hypothesis' in connection with the Corinthian capital. The capitals of Corinthian columns did indeed gradually come to be seen as baskets held in place all round by acanthus leaves.

What is the story? Vitruvius relates that Callimachos, the Corinthian sculptor, once saw a little basket standing on the ground somewhere with acanthus plants growing around its base. So Callimachos, we are told, looked at a little basket surrounded by acanthus leaves and said: 'Here is the Corinthian capital!' Who could imagine anything more materialistic? I will tell you in a moment the real significance of this anecdote narrated by Vitruvius.

The point I am making is that in the course of our modern age all understanding of the inner principle of artistic creation has gradually been lost. If this understanding cannot be rediscovered, people will simply never grasp what we intend by the forms we are creating, such as the forms of our capitals or indeed of our whole building. Those who hold fast to the 'basket' hypothesis will never be able to understand.

The need to rediscover the inner principle of artistic creation

The basis of all artistic creation is to be found in a state of being or consciousness which existed before the beginnings of recorded history. This was a particular consciousness that was active in human beings at the dawn of historical times, and was a remnant of an ancient human clairvoyance. This state of being also belongs to the fourth post-Atlantean epoch, the age of ancient Greece and Rome. Although ancient Egyptian culture belongs to the third post-Atlantean epoch, all that was expressed in Egyptian art belongs to the fourth epoch. By the time of the fourth post-Atlantean epoch this consciousness gave rise to inner feeling in a way that enabled human beings to perceive how human movement, bearing and gestures gave rise to the human form and figure, developing from the etheric into the physical.

To understand what I mean, try to imagine that in those times, when there was a true comprehension of artistic will, the actual sight of a flower or tendril was far less important than the feeling: I have to carry something heavy, I bend my back and generate with my own form the forces that make me, a human being, shape myself in a way that will enable me to bear this weight. Human beings felt within themselves what they had to bring to expression in their own gestures. One movement was used to grip hold of something, while another was an expression of carrying—stretching your hands out in front gives you a feeling that you are carrying something. Out of such gestures arose the lines and shapes leading over into art. Within your own human nature you can sense how the human being can go beyond what eyes see and other senses perceive by becoming a part of the universe as a whole. You take up a position in the universe as a whole when you notice that you cannot just saunter along when carrying something heavy. Out of a feeling for lines of force, which one has to develop inwardly, arises artistic creation. These lines of force are not to be found anywhere in external reality.

The sun and the earth motif in ancient ritual

When engaged in spiritual research one often comes upon a wonderful Akashic picture[2] that depicts a group of human beings uniting as one in an ordered and harmonious way. Imagine a kind of stage surrounded by an amphitheatre filled with spectators. In the centre people are walking round in a procession. This is not supposed to create a naturalistic impression in the spectators but a sense of something lofty or indeed supersensible. Seen from above it would look like this:

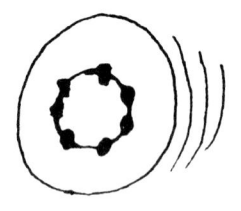

And the side view would show a group of people walking in a circular procession one behind the other, surrounded by the spectators.

The image of these people in procession portrays

Manifestations of Spiritual Realities 83

something of great significance, something that does not exist in the physical world but can only be expressed in analogies. They portray something that brings human beings into connection with the macrocosm. In those times of the ancient world people were concerned to represent the relationship of earthly forces to those of the sun. How can this relationship come to be experienced? It is like the feeling one has when bearing a load. Earthly things rest squarely on the ground, but when they endeavour to wrest themselves free—if you imagine the forces necessary for this—a pointed shape emerges. The human being's state of being bound to the earth is therefore expressed by a shape that has a wide base and runs upwards to a point. Sensing these forces, people felt that they were standing on the earth.

In a similar way they also became aware of their connection with the sun. The sun works downwards towards the earth, and they expressed this by portraying the lines of force raying inwards, just as the sun, in its apparent journey round the earth, sends its rays down towards the earth as a focal point. These two alternating representations give you the earth motif and the sun motif carried in antiquity by the people who formed the circling procession. Round them sat the spectators, and in the centre the actors passed around in procession, alternately one with the earth motif and one with the sun motif — whose incoming rays can also be seen as sun forces radiating outwards and downwards from their source.

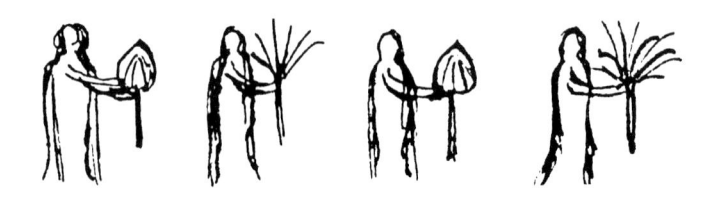

This cosmic tension between earth and sun was initially an inner, feeling experience; only subsequently did people begin to consider how they might portray it. The best medium for the purposes of artistic expression proved to be a plant or tree whose forms run upwards to a point from a wider base, alternating with palms. Plants having a form like a wide bud were alternated with palms. The palms represented the sun forces, and bud-forms running upwards to a point, the earth forces.

The palm chosen as an expression of the sun forces

People learnt to feel their position within the cosmos and created, so to speak, certain form relationships. Subsequently, on reflection, they selected certain plants as a means of expression, instead of creating artistic objects for

Manifestations of Spiritual Realities

the purpose. The choice of suitable plants was the artistically creative act, which was in turn the result of a living experience of cosmic connections. Thus the creative urge in human beings is no mere wish to imitate things in the world around them. The artistic representation of natural things only entered art at a later stage. When people no longer realized that palms were used to express sun forces, they began to think that the ancients had simply imitated palms in their designs. This was never the case—the people of antiquity used the leaves of palms because their form typified the sun forces. All true artistic creation has arisen from a superabundance of forces within the human being—forces that cannot come to full expression in external reality but which we strive to express through our awareness of our connection with the universe as a whole.

In both science and art, a certain misleading and confusing idea is very difficult to erase from people's considerations and perceptions. This is the idea that simple things inevitably give rise to more complex ones. This is untrue. For example, the construction of the human eye is much simpler than that in many lower animals. The course of evolution is actually often from the complex to the simple, so that the most intricate interlacing finally resolves into a straight line. In many instances simplification is the later stage, and we will not acquire a true conception of evolution until we realize this.

Primeval experience condensed to an ornamental motif

What people sensed in those ancient times, and what was presented to the spectators seated round the arena as a depiction of living, cosmic forces was later simplified into ornamental lines summarizing what had once been a living experience. The complexity of human evolution honed down into the simple lines of an ornamental border might be drawn like this:[3]

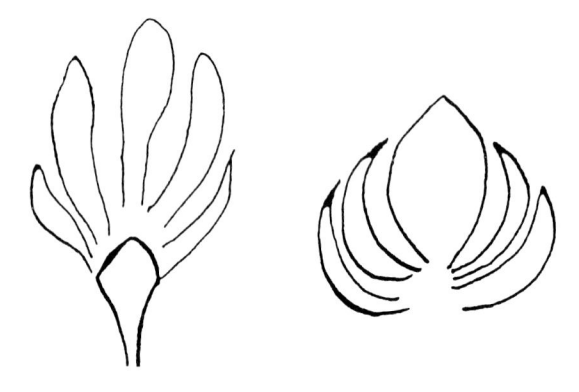

In these alternating patterns you have a simplified reproduction of the people circling in procession with earth motif, sun motif, earth motif, sun motif and so on. What human beings felt and experienced in those ancient times is here summarized in an ornamental border. This decorative motif was already a feature of Mesopotamian art, and it is also found in Greek art as the so-called 'palm

Manifestations of Spiritual Realities 87

motif', either in this form or a similar one, resembling the lotus petal.

This alternation of earth and sun motif presented itself to the artistic feeling of people as a decorative ornamental theme in the truest sense. Later people forgot that in this decorative ornament they were looking at an unconscious reproduction of a very ancient dance gesture, a festive, ceremonial dance. Nonetheless, this fact has been preserved in the 'palm motif'.

The Doric capital

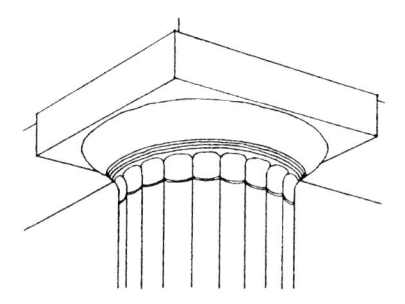

It is interesting to consider the following. Among the painted decorations of some Doric capitals you often find an intriguing motif which I will sketch thus. Beneath the weight borne by the capital is the torus and below that we find the 'palm motif' as a painted theme showing the earth and sun motif in a somewhat modified form encircling the whole top of the column. Above is the Doric torus, and below it, painted right round the top of the column, the ornamental motif as a decoration. In this way some Doric columns actually show the 'palm motif' painted beneath the capital like the procession of alternating earth and sun motifs.

Earth   Sun   Earth

The Ionic capital

In Greece, where the fourth post-Atlantean epoch came to fullest expression, all that came over from Asia, embodied in what I have now described as decorations on Doric columns, became united with the dynamic architectural principle of weight-bearing as such. The fact that this union came about in Greece was due to the 'I' attaining the fullest integration with the human body there, so that this design motif found expression in Greek culture. The 'I', when it is within the body, must grow strong if it has to bear a load. You feel this gesture in the volute:

Manifestations of Spiritual Realities 89

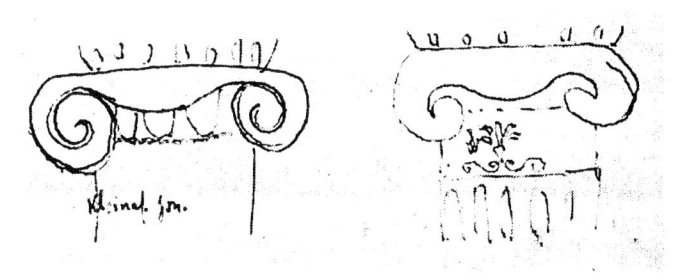

Ionic capitals by Rudolf Steiner, from his notebook, June 1914

It is this feeling of strengthening which we experience in the volute. It was particularly in the fourth post-Atlantean epoch that the human ego was being strengthened; and this is expressed in the volute. Thus we arrive at the basic form of the Ionic capital. It is as though, unseen within the capital, Atlas is bearing the world on his shoulders, and the volute becomes the weight-bearer.

You need only imagine the middle portion, which is merely indicated in the Ionic capital, developing downwards to become the complete volute, and you have the Corinthian capital. The middle portion is simply extended downwards, so that the character of weight-bearing becomes complete. Then think of this weight-bearing expressed in the form of a sculpted figure, and you have human force bent over in itself—the ego force bent over, bearing weight:

Corinthian capitals by Steiner, from his notebook, June 1914

The Corinthian capital

We can speak of an artistic principle when we have a large-scale motif that can be repeated or reproduced in miniature, or vice versa. Imagine the Corinthian capital with the main volute bearing the abacus, and repeat this artistic motif lower down where it only serves as an ornament. The result all the way round the base of the capital is a sculptural reproduction of the whole thing as a decoration. Now imagine the painting on the Doric capital, which grew out of the decorative representation of a very ancient motif, being united with the sculptural decoration on the Corinthian capital. Imagine sensing the wish to recreate in relief what used to be only painted, and

Manifestations of Spiritual Realities   91

Corinthian capital with acanthus leaves

you will find the painted motif reappearing in relief form. I can illustrate this for you with the diagram of the palm motif. The urge arose to bring the 'palm motif' into the later decorative motif. Here [*in the Corinthian capital*] it was not a motif representing the bearing of a load; what was mere painting in the Doric capital, and therefore flat, was sculpted in the Corinthian capital, and the palm leaves were made to turn downwards. On the left I have drawn a 'palm motif', and below it the beginning which arises when the 'palm motif' is worked out in relief. If I were to continue, the painted Doric 'palm motif' would metamorphose into the Corinthian sculpted 'palm motif'. The 'palm motif' when sculpted becomes the so-called acanthus leaf.

The acanthus leaf arises when the 'palm motif' is

worked out in relief. It is the result of an urge not to paint the 'palm motif' but to work it out, to sculpt it in high relief. The weight-bearing aspect became increasingly elaborate until it began to give people the feeling that it resembled the acanthus leaf, and so this is what they came to call it, although it has nothing to do with any such thing. Thus the whole nonsense about the motif being a naturalistic representation of an acanthus leaf is exposed. What is now called the acanthus leaf did not arise out of naturalistic representation at all, but out of a metamorphosis of the ancient sun motif, the 'palm motif', being sculpted instead of painted. So you see that these artistic forms have arisen from an *inner* perception of gestures within the human etheric body, the flowing lines of force connected with every movement.

Art cannot arise by imitation of the external world

Art in its essence can no more arise from an imitation of nature than music can be created by imitating nature. Indeed even when art is imitative, the thing that is imitated is fundamentally secondary, an accessory, and thus naturalism in itself is absolutely contrary to true artistic feeling. If the shapes and forms in our art here[4] are thought by others to be grotesque, we will be able to draw comfort from the knowledge that the artistic conceptions that find our art grotesque are those that see in the acanthus motif nothing but a naturalistic imitation. In reality it is drawn from the spirit and only in its later development came to bear a remote resemblance to the acanthus leaf. Artistic comprehension in future ages will simply be unable to understand this attitude of mind which in our time influences not only the art experts, who are supposed to understand their subject, but which also dominates artistic creation as such. The materialistic attitude of mind in Darwinism also confronts us in artistic creation where there is a growing tendency to turn art into a mere imitation of nature. Insight into the origin of the acanthus motif has given me much joy, for it proves circumstantially that the primordial forms of artistic creation have also sprung from the human soul and not from imitation of external phenomena.

Understanding art comes from doing art

I was only really able to penetrate to the essence of art after I had myself created the forms of our building here. Feeling the forms, moulding them out of the very wellsprings of human development, leads to a sense of how artistic creation has arisen in human evolution. It is a remarkable karmic situation that during the time when I was deeply engaged in pursuing a certain artistic intuition, which had arisen during the General Meeting in Berlin in 1912, I began to investigate what I had created in these forms in order to arrive at a deeper understanding of them. This was after the forms of our building had already been designed. You can only think afterwards about artistic forms. If you understand them first and then carry them out they will be of no use at all; if you create on the basis of concepts and ideas nothing of value will ensue. The very thing that I perceived so clearly in connection with the acanthus leaf, and what I proved to be erroneous about it, is an indication of the inner connections between the spiritual science which will be active within our building and those things which it will express artistically.

Alois Riegl on the origins of the Corinthian capital

Just occasionally there are signs that these things are also understood elsewhere. Alois Riegl appears to have reached the same conclusion, that the so-called acanthus leaf developed from the 'palm motif', though he failed to realize that 'palm motif', too, is merely a word behind which the reality of the sun-earth motif is hidden. He referred to the Vitruvian anecdote about Callimachos but omitted to say that the basket Callimachos saw was on the grave of a young girl. By mentioning this location Vitruvius was implying that Callimachos was a clairvoyant who saw above the girl's grave the sun forces struggling with the earth forces, and above this the girl herself floating in her pure etheric body. Here we have a hint of how the sun-earth motif came to be depicted on a capital. By seeing with clairvoyance what is actually present above the grave of a young girl you can come to under-

Manifestations of Spiritual Realities 95

stand how the 'palm motif' can be transformed into the acanthus leaf. It grows up all around the ether body of the young virgin, which rises up in accordance with the sun laws. The same is depicted in the 'Clytie' portrait showing the bust of a noble Roman woman, which appears to be growing out of a flower. This is a late Roman statue showing what a clairvoyant may see above the graves of certain people.

'Clytie', portrait of a Roman woman c.AD40

We shall not understand what really underlies the anecdote quoted by Vitruvius until we have outgrown the unfortunate habit of asking what everything means and of always looking for symbolic interpretations showing how this, that or the other depicts the physical body, the ether body or the astral body. Once this habit has been eradicated from our movement we shall come to understand what really underlies artistic form. It is either a direct perception of how one moves spiritually or it is a perception of the corresponding etheric movement.[5]

6. Metamorphosis in Architecture

As we saw in chapter 5, Steiner's aesthetics were founded on Goethe's concept of art as a revelation of the 'secret laws of nature'. One of the most fundamental of these laws, which Goethe researched through his method of observation but which can also be explored by artistic means, is the phenomenon of metamorphosis.

Metamorphosis is a time process that Goethe saw as the basis of plant morphology, weather patterns and indeed virtually all processes of development and change in the field of life sciences.[1] Steiner extended this research into the field of 'spiritual science' and discovered that the laws of metamorphosis lie behind many phenomena, including the phases of human life and, indeed, the entire evolution of the cosmos from 'Old Saturn' onwards (see Introduction and chapter 1).

If a new architecture is to make spiritual forces visible in matter then the principles of metamorphosis must become one of its central elements. Thus Steiner attempted to introduce a time process *into the* spatial *language of architecture. He worked with metamorphosis in both of his Goetheanum buildings in a number of ways.*

The best-known example of Steiner's artistic work with metamorphosis is the capitals and bases of the two sequences of columns in the two circular spaces of the first building. In the first passage reproduced here Steiner gives an explanation of the

98   Architecture

sequence of seven capitals incorporated in the larger space. His essay relates to the original version of the sequence, which was a series of painted boards, alternating with a second sequence of pictures based on the Apocalypse, referred to as 'seals' by Steiner. These were placed around the edge of a conference hall in Munich during the 1907 Congress of the world Theosophical Society, hosted by the German Section of which Steiner was the General Secretary at the time.[2] This was his first attempt to introduce architecture as an aspect of esoteric work. As he said, 'The Munich Congress was intended to bear witness to something that I have again and again stressed with regard to our theosophical impulse. It was to show that theosophy is not only a matter of personal brooding and introspection. Theosophy should make an impact on practical life ... [and should be] a matter of involvement in all branches of practical existence.'[3]

In the second passage reproduced here, Steiner discusses Goethe's research on metamorphosis in the skeleton[4] and goes on to talk about the relationship between the first building and its boiler house.

The columns at Munich 1907

Note: The illustrations used here are photographs of the column capitals in the more developed form in which they were executed in the first Goetheanum building.

Alternating with the seals in the Congress Hall were the seven columns reproduced in the second series of illustrations. As already indicated above, these represent experiences of the 'seer' (which is no longer a suitable term here)[5] in the 'spiritual world'. What is represented here are primordial forces consisting of spiritual tones. The sculptural forms of the capitals are translations of what the 'seer' hears. Yet these forms are by no means arbitrary; they arise in a quite objective manner when the 'seeing human being' allows the 'spiritual music' (harmony of the spheres) streaming through his whole being to work through the creative, shaping faculty of his hand. The sculptural forms are here really a kind of 'frozen music' that manifests the secrets of the universe.

The fact that these forms appear as the capitals of columns is self-explanatory to one who understands the situation. The foundation of the physical evolution of all earthly beings lies in the spiritual world. It is 'supported' from there. Now *all* evolution depends upon a progression in seven stages. (The number seven should not be regarded as the result of 'superstition' but as the expression of a spiritual law, just as the colours of the rainbow are the expression of a physical law.) The earth itself progresses in its evolution through seven states that are designated by the names of the seven planets: Saturn, Sun, Moon, Mars, Mercury, Jupiter, Venus conditions.[6] Not only a heavenly body progresses in this way, but *every* development takes its course in seven stages, which in modern spiritual science are called by the names of the seven planetary conditions. As explained above, the spiritual forces of support that maintain these conditions are revealed by the forms of the column capitals.

It is however impossible properly to understand the matter in hand if one confines oneself to an intellectual explanation whilst looking at the forms. One must contemplate these forms with *artistic sensibility* and allow the capitals to exert their effect on one as *form*. Whoever disregards this will imagine he is only confronted by allegories or at best by symbols. Then he would have misunderstood everything. The same *motif* (or theme) goes through all seven capitals: a force from above, and a force from below, that first of all strive towards each other, then, reaching each other work together. The fullness and inner life of these forces have to be *felt* and then the soul itself has to *experience* how, shaping themselves in a living way, they spread, draw together, embrace or clasp each other, entwine or engulf each other, open up or unfold and so on. It is possible to feel this complexity of the forces in the same way one feels the 'self-shaping' of the plant out of its vital forces, and one can sense how the line of force first of all goes up vertically in the column, how it unfolds below in the sculpted shapes of the capitals that open themselves up towards the forces approaching them from above, so that a meaningfully supporting capital may arise.

First of all the force from below unfolds in the simplest way and the force from above strives towards it in equal simplicity (Saturn column); then the forms from above fill out, thrust their way into the forms from below and cause

Metamorphosis in Architecture 101

Saturn column

the lower forms to give way to the sides. At the same time the lower forms open up as living shapes (Sun column).

Subsequently the upper part becomes more manifold, a point that had pushed forth grows out into a fertilizing principle, and the lower part transforms itself into a fruit bearer. The other *motif* of force between the two has become a steadying support, bearer or bracket, because the relationship of the intermediate members would otherwise not be experienced as stable and strong enough (Moon column).

A separation between the lower and upper regions now takes place. The strong bearers of the Moon capital have

Sun column

Metamorphosis in Architecture 103

Moon column

Mars column

themselves become column-like, the upper and lower members between them have fused into a single figure, a *new motif* is indicated from above (Mars column).

The shapes that have arisen out of the connection between the upper and lower elements have taken on life, and appear therefore as a staff entwined by serpents. One will have to feel how this *motif* grows organically out of the foregoing. The central forms of the Mars capital have disappeared; their force has been absorbed by the supporting interior parts of the capital. The previous indications from above have filled out (Mercury column).

A kind of simplification now develops that nevertheless contains within it the fruit of the former complexity (manifoldness or articulation). The upper part opens up like a chalice, the lower part simplifies its life in a chaste[7] form (Jupiter column).

The final stage shows the 'inner fullness' accompanying the outward simplification to the highest degree. The transformations of growth from below have drawn forth from above a chalice-like shape with a fruit-bearing form (Venus column).

Whoever can sense what comes to expression in these pillars of world evolution *feels* comprehensive laws of all existence that solve the riddles of life in quite a different manner from abstract 'natural laws'.

In these designs a sample is offered of the way spiritual perception can become form, life, artistic image. It should be held in mind that the illustrations reproduce living forces of existence of the higher worlds and these higher

106 Architecture

Mercury column

Metamorphosis in Architecture 107

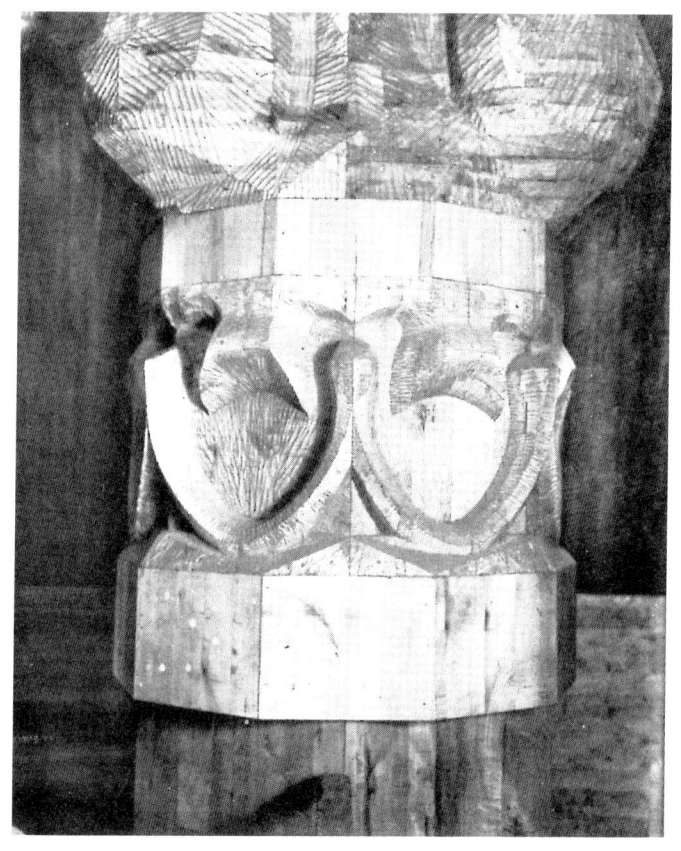

Jupiter column

108 ARCHITECTURE

Venus column

spiritual forces *work* deeply upon the beholder of the pictures. They work directly upon corresponding forces that slumber in every human being. But their effect is only right if one contemplates these pictures in the right inner frame of mind. One who looks at the pictures with theosophic ideas in his head and theosophic feelings in his heart will receive the holiest impressions from them. But if one were to hang or to place them in an unsuitable place where they are experienced with everyday trivial thoughts and feelings, one will notice an unfavourable effect that can go so far as to have an injurious influence upon our physical life. One is advised to act accordingly and only to seek a relationship with the pictures that is in harmony with a reverence for the spiritual worlds. Such pictures *ought* to serve as decoration for a room serving the higher life. But one should not find them or contemplate them in places where people's thoughts do not accord with them.[8]

The Goetheanum boiler-house

I should like to begin today by saying a few words about the boiler-house attached to the Goetheanum and the architectural principle underlying it. If you want to study what motivated the architectural forms of this house, you must bear in mind that it is part of the whole Goetheanum building and belongs to it. This fact of it belonging to the building has to come to expression in the artistic concep-

110   Architecture

The first Goetheanum from the north-east with the boiler-house in the foreground

tion of the building itself, if this conception is correct. It should not be an abstraction but has to be expressed in the artistic form.

Now let us have a look at the whole question of related artistic forms. We get closest to this if we do what human beings unfortunately do far too seldom, and think of the tremendous artistic creative activity we find exemplified if we are able to look at the spiritual aspect of nature and recognize natural creation as a product of the spirit. I would like to draw your attention to the forms of the bony system because it is easiest to see there. Man's skeletal system, especially, is easier to study than the forms of other living organisms.

Goethe's work on the metamorphosis of the skeleton

You will know that I have been trying for decades to arouse some understanding in the world for the significant discoveries Goethe made in the field of anatomy and physiology, which I should like to call his second major achievement in this realm. I will not touch on the first one today but only refer to the second. This second significant discovery owes its origin to what one might, in the external materialistic world, call the combination of chance and human genius. Goethe himself relates that one day when he was going for a walk in the Jewish cemetery in Venice he found a sheep's skull that had fallen apart at the seams. Picking it up and looking at the form of the bones the thought occurred to him, 'When I look at these head bones, what actually are they? They are transformed dorsal vertebrae.'

You know, of course, that the spinal cord enclosing the spine marrow as a nerve cord is composed of rings which fit into one another, rings with a definite shape and processes (*procesus vertebralis*). And if you imagine one of these rings expanding so that the hole the marrow passes through—for the rings fit into one another—begins to get larger and the bone gets correspondingly thinner and expands like elastic, not only in a horizontal direction but also in other directions, then the form that arises out of this ring form is nothing else but the bone formation which forms our skull. Our skulls are transformed dorsal vertebrae.

On the basis of spiritual science we can develop this discovery of Goethe's even further and can say today that every bone man has is a transformation, a metamorphosis of a single form. The only reason we do not notice this is because we have very primitive views of what can arise through transformation. If you think of a bone of the upper arm—you know of course what it looks like—a tubular bone like that would not immediately strike you as being similar to a bone in our head. But that is only due to us not having a sufficiently developed concept of transformation.

The first idea you will have is that the tubular bone has to be puffed up until it is hollow inside, then you ought to arrive at the form of the head bone. But that is not the principle underlying the shapes of the bones. A tubular bone would first have to be turned round, and you would not see the similarity it has to the skull-cap until you had turned it inside out like a glove. But when a person turns a glove inside out he expects it to look the same as it did before, doesn't he? This is because the glove is something dead. It is quite different with something living. If the glove were alive, the following would happen when it was turned inside out. Changes would occur like the thumb and the little finger getting very long, the middle finger very short, and the palm contracting, and so on. The turning inside out and the varying elasticity of the material would bring about all sorts of changes, in fact the glove would acquire a totally different form, although it would still be a glove. This is how you must imagine a tubular upper arm bone being turned inside out, so that a skull emerges.

The principle of metamorphosis based on a primary form

You will realize that the wise powers of the Godhead in the cosmos possessed a greater wisdom than we human beings—who think ourselves superior—have today, to be able to set the forces of transformation in motion that are needed to form a skull. The inner unity in nature comes from the very fact that, fundamentally, even the most dissimilar forms are transformations of one archetypal form. There is nothing in the realm of life that could not arise as a metamorphosis of a primary form. In the course of this metamorphosis something else happens as well. Certain parts of the primary form become larger at the expense of others, and other parts become smaller; also various limbs expand, but not all to the same extent. This produces dissimilarities, although they are all transformations of the same primary form.

The Goetheanum boiler-house as a metamorphosis of the main building

Now look at the primary form of our whole Goetheanum building. I can only give you a very sketchy account of

114 ARCHITECTURE

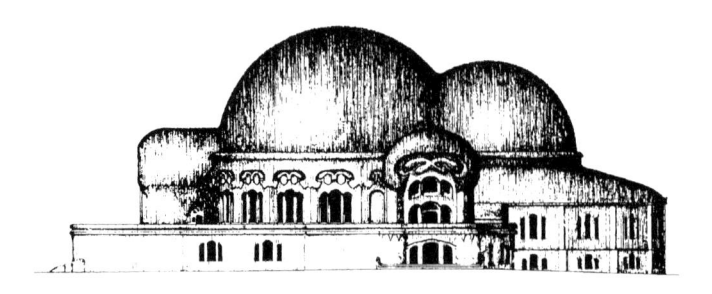

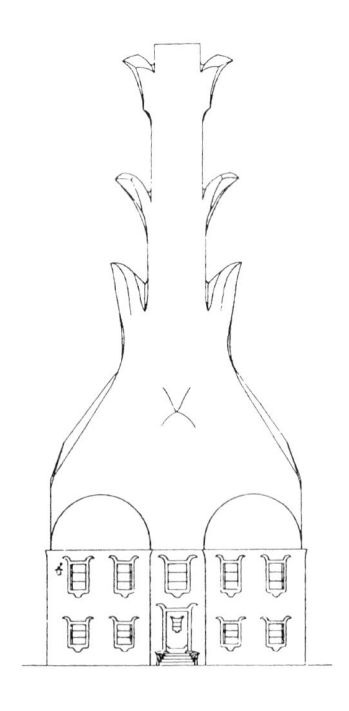

Metamorphosis in Architecture 115

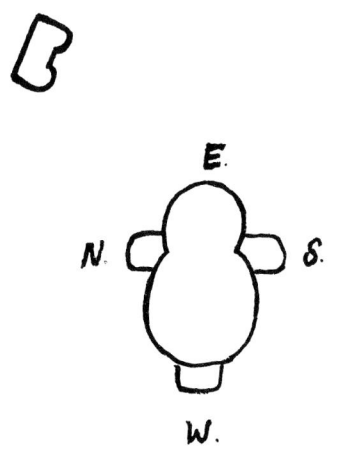

what I want to tell you, and only mention one point of view. If you look at the Goetheanum you will see that it has double domes and that the domes rest on a cylindrical substructure. The fact that it is a building with double domes is vital, for these double domes are an expression of the living element. If there had only been one dome then in essence our building would have been dead. The living quality of our building is expressed in the fact that the consciousness of the one dome is reflected in the other, as it were, that the two domes mirror one another, just as the exterior part of the human being is reflected in his organs. The basic concept of the double dome must be borne in mind in relation to anything organically connected with the Goetheanum, for if it were not to contain the double dome form, however hard it was to recognize, it would not express the essential nature of the concept of the building. Therefore the annexe must also contain the concept of the double dome.

Now look at the double dome and its additional constructions. First of all we have the interpenetration of the two dome motifs, whose importance I have often referred to. They represent a kind of innovation in architecture and, as you know, were done with the help of Herr Englert. The interpenetration of the two domes is of special importance in the main building because it expresses the inner connection of the two elements which mirror one another. I am giving you this concept of mirroring in an abstract way at the moment. A very great deal is contained in this interpenetration of the two dome motifs—an infinite number of different aspects. The further stage of the building, the artistic stage, that expresses as image the concept of spiritual science can only come into being because we have succeeded in achieving this interpenetration of the double dome motifs. So we have this interpenetration in the main building. If we were to cancel the interpenetration and separate the dome motifs, we move towards the ahrimanic[9] principle. If we bring them closer together or overlap them completely, by building one inside the other, we would approach the luciferic principle.

So the ahrimanic principle has to be removed from the Goetheanum. In the boiler-house the domes have to be pushed apart, for in the case of this building as well, the dome concept is vital. And now imagine the domes kept

Metamorphosis in Architecture 117

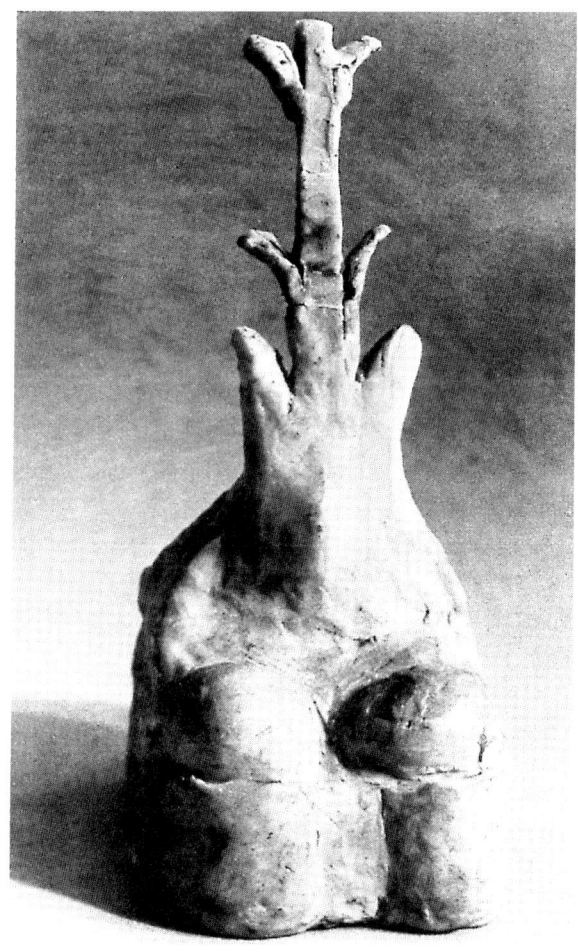

Steiner's wax model of the boiler-house, which he was referring to in his talk

apart. Imagine that on one side, this side motif [*south portal of the main building*] has shrunk to nothing, so the dotted line has gone; and on the other side it has grown considerably larger [*and become the chimney*]. With the main building in mind, imagine that here [*south*] you have the separated domes, here is a front structure, and here the whole thing has been pushed in [*see A*]. There [*B*] the whole thing has been pulled out instead of being pushed in; but here [*A*] it has shrunk to nothing instead of growing. Imagine that on the other side [*the front structure of the north portal*] it developed considerably, and you have the transformation motif for an annexe of our main building which has developed out of the primary forms. For if you imagine this [*the chimney*] getting smaller and smaller, that [*A*] coming out again, and the whole thing pushed together, then the boiler-house would be transformed into the main building.

[*Steiner was using his model of the boiler-house as he spoke.*]

The point is that this metamorphosis of our main building will be suitable for the purpose of its annexe, the boiler-house. Just as a vertebra arises out of the same primary form as the human skull, and you can think of one changing into the other, you can also think of the main building and the annexe changing from one to the other. The concept of the form can pass from one form to the other, if it metamorphoses and becomes alive.

We really have to become apprentices of the creative hierarchies who created by means of metamorphosis, and learn to do the same thing ourselves.

Metamorphosis in Architecture   119

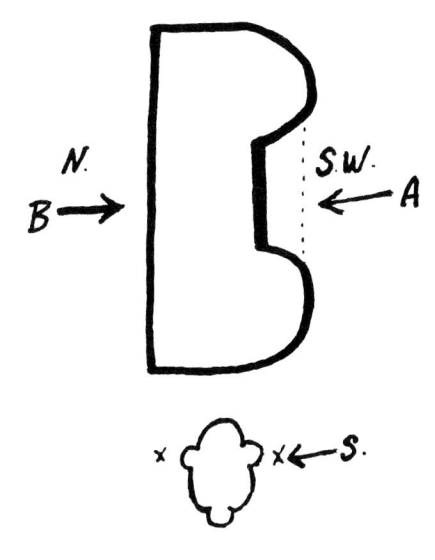

Now imagine the kind of force necessary to enlarge this insignificant looking part on this side [*north portal of the main building which becomes the chimney – see diagrammatic plan at the beginning of this section*]. If you have a small rubber bag that you want to enlarge, you have to press it this way and that way from inside so that it gets bigger. A force has to be there that can enlarge things and develop them. So if one of these side wings really has to be puffed up, it would have to be done by a force working from inside, from here.

What kind of forces can they be, in there? You can study these forces in the forms of the architraves.[10] If you imagine the forces in the architraves jumping into the side structure and pushing the north portal up, you get this form [*chimney and back wall*]. You have to try and slip inside these forms of the architraves with your formative artistic thinking and contract and expand them. Imagine that because you have slipped inside, you enlarge what is small in there. Then this form arises [*chimney and back wall*]. There is no other way of going about creating things that belong together than by trying to get inside them.

This slipping into things and being inside them is another way of imitating the creative forces in nature, and unless modern industrial civilization does this it will not overcome its shallow and materialistic approach. It would be impossible to imagine the ordinary kind of chimney as a product of natural creation. It only exists because there is a denial of divine-spiritual forces in nature. There is hardly anything outside in nature that you could compare with an ordinary chimney except possibly the rather hideous-looking asparagus plant. But that is a kind of exception. Whatever grows with the forces of earth can never go straight upwards like a chimney. If you want to study the forces that work in an upwards direction, a tree is the best example in which to find what corresponds to the hidden forces in the earth. For a tree does not only develop a trunk in the vertical, but also has to reach outwards with its branches. The point obviously is not to imitate this directly in the model, but to study those forces which radiate out from the earth and overcome the purely vertical direction of the tree trunk by reaching out breadthways and putting forth branches.

Although I have only been able to show you the roughest principles, I could justify the principles behind this architectural form in minute detail in the case of every single plane, but it would take us too long.

Now a form such as this is only complete when fulfilling its purpose. If you look at the form now it is not complete. It will only be complete when the heating is actually functioning inside and smoke is coming out; smoke belongs to it, it really belongs, and this has been included in the architectural form. One day the rising of smoke will be observed clairvoyantly, and the smoke coming out of the chimney, the spiritual part of the rising smoke, will also be taken into consideration. For we shall know, when we have really observed it clairvoyantly, that the physical also contains a spiritual element.

For just as you have a physical, an etheric and an astral body, the smoke also has at least an etheric part. And this

122 Architecture

Metamorphosis in Architecture 123

etheric part goes a different way from the physical. The physical part will go upwards, but the etheric part is really caught by these little shoots that reach outwards. A time will come when people will see the physical part of the smoke rising while the etheric part wafts away. When we express this kind of thing in form, we are beginning to comply with a principle of all art, namely, the presenting of inner essence in outer form, really making inner essence the principle according to which an outer form is created.

As I said, I would have to do a lot of talking if I were to go into all the details on which these architectural forms are based, although these might be far more interesting than those we have already discussed. One of these interesting things is that it was possible to express everything that had to be expressed in this modern material, and build with concrete. For it will be possible to go a long way with form-making in this modern material, especially in the designing of buildings in this style that will serve modern, ahrimanic civilization.[11] In fact it is essential to do so.

There is no need for me to go into any further details, because I am more concerned with showing you the principle of this building and everything to do with it. This principle can be modified in many respects. For instance the dome can be modified so that it does not look like a dome any more, if it is looked at merely from the geometrical-mathematical point of view and not organically, and so on. But today I wanted to discuss the particular principles of inner essence and transformation, the life principle within these. I wanted to cite this to show you in what way real artistic creativity, when it has to do with our spiritual-scientific conception, has to differ from any kind of symbolic interpretation, for that is external. It is a matter of getting an inner grasp of what you are being shown here and following the process with your whole soul.[12]

7. Aspects of a New Architecture

In the first passage quoted here from a lecture given in 1915 Steiner refers to the potential of architecture to incorporate sculpture, painting and coloured glass into a synthesis in which architecture and sculpture take on musical qualities.[1] Goethe's statement about architecture being 'frozen music' comes to mind, but Steiner, having incorporated the time process of metamorphosis into architecture, has moved this question onto another level. He has gone beyond the use of mathematical proportion and the 'harmony of the spheres', which music and classical architecture can be said to have in common. With metamorphosis he started to work with spatial equivalents of musical intervals and theme development, notably in the series of columns in the first Goetheanum.

If the intervals between the columns are what give them their musical quality, these spaces become as significant as the columns themselves. In the next passage, the first of several taken from a lecture given in 1914, Steiner talks about negative space as the underlying principle behind the whole interior of the first Goetheanum and refers to this as being like a jelly mould: '. . . the living negative of the words that are spoken and the deeds that are done in the building'.

Steiner goes on from this to discuss the sculptural quality of the relief carving of the 'living walls' of the building and their connection with the relief of the earth's surface.

In the following passage Steiner talks about the coloured windows in the Goetheanum buildings, in which a new technique was employed of cutting into thick coloured glass (using power tools) and thereby producing different levels of light and darkness. Apart from the coloured light from the windows themselves, coloured shadows were produced where the light fell onto the columns within the space, as happens today in the second Goetheanum.

In the last passage from this 1914 lecture Steiner discusses the potentially moral influence that art and architecture can have in the future, making peace talks and external regulations redundant because peace and harmony will be embodied in the forms themselves.

Finally, we return to the subject of colour and architecture with a talk given in 1911 at the dedication of a new building for the Anthroposophical Society in Stuttgart.[2] Here Steiner talks about how the activity for which a space is intended can be supported by an appropriate colour or, alternatively, hindered by an inappropriate one. The reason for this, he says, is that different colours and different applications of colours (such as opaque and transparent) bring us into connection with different spiritual beings through their effect on our etheric body.

Architecture as a new synthesis of the arts

Reconciling the arts—that is what we attempted to do, for the first time, and in a small, elementary way, in our Goetheanum building. We did not want only to talk in a

Aspects of a New Architecture

Looking from the auditorium to the stage in the first Goetheanum

cold, abstract way about it, but show in the architecture of the building itself an impression, a copy of this reconciling of a musical mood with architectural form. If you study what is presented in our series of pillars and everything connected with them, you will discover that we were making the attempt to bring the elements of support, weight and balance into living movement. Our pillars are not merely supports, our capitals no longer mere supporting devices, and the architraves that extend above the pillars do not just have the character of rest, serving only to round the pillars off at the top, but they have a character of living growth and movement.

We attempted to bring architectural forms into musical flux, and the feeling one can have from seeing the interplay between the pillars and all that is connected with them can of itself arouse a musical mood in the soul. It will be possible to feel invisible music as the soul of the columns and the architectural and sculptural forms that belong to them. It is as though a soul element were in them. And the interpenetration of the fine arts and their forms by musical moods must be the fundamental ideal of the art of the future. Music of the future will be more sculptural than music of the past. Architecture and sculpture of the future will be more musical than they were in the past. That will be the essential thing. Yet this will not stop music from being an independent art. On the contrary, it will become ever richer through penetrating the secrets of the tones, as we said yesterday, creating musical forms out of the spiritual foundations of the cosmos.

Aspects of a New Architecture

Sequence of seven columns (from right to left) and architrave as interpreted for the completion of the auditorium of the second Goetheanum by Christian Hitsch and PA Wolf, 1997

However, as everything that is inside must also be outside — all that lives in art must be embodied in a kind of organism — the world of soul within the series of pillars and everything belonging to them must also be embodied. This happens or at least is about to happen in the painting of the domes. Just as the pillars and everything belonging to them are, as it were, the body of our building, so all that is going to appear in the domes — when you are inside the building — is its soul; and in the same way that the world appears filled with spirit to our outward-directed organs of perception, so our windows executed in the new art of glass shading shall represent the spirit. Body, soul and spirit will be expressed in our building. Body in the column structure, soul in everything to do with the domes, and spirit in what is in the windows.[3]

Surfaces formed by and reflecting the word — the jelly-mould principle

In trying to understand the principle of the interior space formed by our two half domes, or, more correctly, three-quarter domes, we could do worse than imagine how a jelly-mould works. The jelly takes shape inside the mould and when the mould is upturned and removed, the jelly reveals all the forms that are present in negative inside the mould:

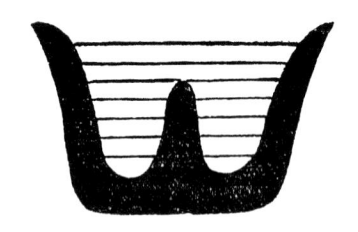

The same principle may be applied in the case of the interior design of our building, only here there is no jelly inside but the living word of spiritual science moving and weaving in the form possible for it. All that is enclosed within the spatial shapes, all that is spoken here and done within them, must adapt to them as the jelly adapts to the negative forms of the jelly-mould. We should feel the walls as the living negative of the words that are spoken and the deeds that are done in the building. That is the principle of the interior design here. Think of the living words of spiritual science as they encounter these walls,

Aspects of a New Architecture 131

hollowing them out in accordance with their profundity of meaning. They hollow out shapes that fit their meaning. This is why these interior forms are shaped as they are, worked out of the flat surface.[4]

Living walls

However many columns there are in a Greek temple, the whole is nonetheless governed by gravity. In our building,

The rear of the auditorium showing columns, capitals, bases and architrave

however, nothing is mere wall. The essential thing is that forms grow out of the wall. When the time comes for us to walk about inside our building we shall find many sculpted forms, a continuous relief joining the capitals, and other forms on plinths and architraves. What is their significance? It is that they grow out of the wall, and the wall is their soil without which they could not exist.

In the interior of our building there will be a great deal of such relief carving in wood: of forms which, although they are not to be found elsewhere in the physical world, represent an onward flowing evolution. Beginning with a few forceful 'musical phrases' between the Saturn columns at the back, there will be a kind of symphonic progression of harmonies culminating in a finale in the east of the building. But these forms are no more present in the outer physical world than are melodies. These forms are walls that have come alive. Physical walls do not come alive, but etheric walls, spiritual walls do indeed come alive.

The earth's surface as relief

There is a relief in existence which is full of meaning, only we cannot normally see it. It is a relief based on the right concepts: that the surface of the wall reveals what it depicts. This relief is the surface of the earth itself, including its plant cover. In order to study this properly, however, we would have to step out into space and look

Aspects of a New Architecture 133

back at its surface from there. [*This is before space travel of course! — Ed.*] The earth is the living surface that brings forth shapes. This is what our relief is to be like, giving us a clear sense that the wall is alive, just as we know that the earth is alive and can bring forth the plant world from its depths. Then we shall have achieved a genuine art of relief. To do more than this would be to sin against the essential nature of the relief. Looking down at the great relief of the earth we see people and animals moving upon it, but they do not belong to the relief. Of course we could include them in the relief, since the arts can be developed in all directions, but in essence it would then no longer be a pure art of relief.

Re-connecting with paradise

Through the forms in its interior our building must speak in the language of the gods. Think for a moment of human beings living on the actual surface of the earth. We need not even draw on our spiritual science but can simply turn to the legend of Paradise. If human beings had remained in Paradise they would have looked from outside upon the wonderful relief of the earth with its flora.[5] Instead, they were transplanted down to the earth where they now live within the relief without being able to see it from outside. They have departed from Paradise and the speech of the gods cannot reach them because the speech of the earth is louder and drowns it. If we pay heed to the organs of the gods which they themselves created when, as Elohim, they gave the earth to man; if we pay heed to the etheric forms of the plants and mould our walls in accordance with them, then—just as nature created the larynx in human beings in order that they might speak— we are indeed creating larynxes through which the gods may speak to us. When we listen attentively to the forms in our walls, which are larynxes for the gods, we are seeking the way back to Paradise.

Coloured glass windows

I now want to indicate how our glass windows are to unite outside with inside. Each window will be of one colour, but there will be different colours at different places, expressing the way the interplay between outside and inside must have a spiritual harmony. Within each monochrome window there will be thicker and thinner parts—parts where the physical substance is thicker, more solid, and parts where it is thinner. More light will shine in through the thinner parts and less through the thicker ones, which will thus yield darker shades. The interplay between spirit and matter will be sensed in what the windows express; and the whole of the interior surface will strive to be an organ for the speech of the gods. The larynx makes it possible for human beings to speak, and in the same way we shall sense that the whole shaping in relief of our building's interior is an organ with which the gods can speak to us from all directions of the universe. Everywhere there are speech organs of the gods.

What are we aiming for in seeking to make our walls permeable, in seeking to shape them in such a way that they negate themselves so that we can find a way of passing through them by making them into organs of speech for the gods? Our aim is none other than to show that we are searching for the path to the spirit by breaking through our walls and letting the gods use them as organs of speech. When we look at our windows they will tell us in the light and dark shading of their colours: 'Find thus, O Man, the path to the spirit!'

By these means we shall see how the soul is related to the spiritual world when, in sleep at night, it lives outside the body. We shall see how the disembodied soul is related to the spiritual world between death and a new birth. The windows will show us how human beings approaching the threshold of the spiritual world become aware of the abyss. The stations on the path to the spiritual world will be revealed; they will arise like shapes of light, shining in from the western side and revealing to us the mysteries of initiation. We are trying to create walls, the forms of which make the walls themselves seem to dissolve. The pictures in the windows must show us how we are 'breaking through' the walls. They must show us the beings we shall encounter when we search for the path to the spiritual worlds or when we tread it unconsciously; they must show us the attitude we ought to have towards the spiritual worlds.

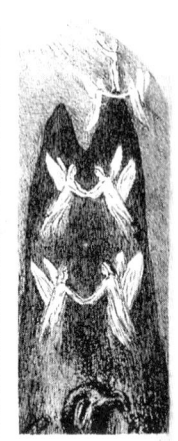

Design for the west window in the first Goetheanum

In earlier times people built the Greek temple as a dwelling place for the god. Later on they built a dwelling place for the congregation seeking union with their god. Both were intended to enclose what was within and exclude what lived outside. Our building will not exclude. Its walls must live and express the truth in their reliefs. The reliefs must express the experience we would have had of the living relief of the plant world if we had not been driven out of Paradise. We would have seen the living relief to which the earth gives birth in the forms of plants; we would have seen what emerges from the geo-

Aspects of a New Architecture 137

logical structures of the mountains, which are only bare where it is right and proper for them to be bare. Sitting there inside our building we must feel that we can be at rest and that then the gods can speak to us. But when the moment comes for us to move on from this state of repose, in which the gods speak to us, to a sense that we ourselves want to become inwardly active in finding the path to the gods, then we have to break through the wall. When this happens we must know what we have to do once we are within the spiritual world. So when we break through the walls the windows must be there to show our soul how to move towards the path that leads to the places from which came the speech brought to us by the forms of the walls. Our feeling must be that sitting here we are surrounded by the organs of speech of the spiritual world. We must want to learn how to understand the language spoken by the forms in such a way that we understand it with our hearts and not through merely intellectual interpretations.

True art and architecture as lawgivers

We will now pass to something else that is closely related to this. A great many buildings have been erected in our time by brilliant architects, and some of them are certainly creations of architectural genius. But they all have one thing in common. We may admire them from outside and think them beautiful inside, but they do not make us feel that we are encompassed in the way we are encompassed by our own sense organs. The reason for this is that these buildings are mute—they do not speak. I would like to elaborate on this tonight.

Let us observe buildings that express all the characteristics of our time. We experience people passing in and out without in any way being able to unite with the architecture, the forms or the artistic conception. We experience that what ought to be expressed through the artistic forms has to be communicated to people by other means instead. In our present time we see an increasing need to use external laws, external regulations and institutions, all of which fall under the heading of 'decrees', to create order, security, peace and harmony. This statement implies no syllable or thought of criticism, since this is how things have to be in our time. But something must be added to this, something that signifies the onward evolution of humanity in a different sense. It is unlikely that all this will be achieved by our building, for we are only making a modest beginning. But we shall have fulfilled the task set us by the gods if, in the future, human culture is able to adopt what is expressed in our building and develop it further. If the ideas underlying such works of architecture find followers in human culture, then people who enter such buildings and allow themselves to take in what speaks through artistic expression, and who learn to understand its language with their heart, and not only with their intellect, will never wrong their fellow human beings. The artistic forms will teach them how to love. They will learn to live with their fellows in peace and harmony. Peace and harmony will pour into hearts through these forms. Such buildings will be 'lawgivers'. And their forms will achieve what external measures can never achieve.

Art and architecture as the larynx of the gods

However much study may be devoted to the elimination of crime and wrongdoing in the world, true redemption, the turning of evil into good, will in future depend upon whether true art and architecture are able to generate a definite cultural atmosphere, an atmosphere that can so fill the hearts and souls of human beings — if they allow this atmosphere to influence them — that liars will cease to lie and disturbers of the peace will cease to disturb the peace of their fellow citizens. Buildings will begin to speak. They will speak a language of which people today have as yet no inkling.

Nowadays people gather at congresses to negotiate world peace. They imagine that speaking and listening can actually create peace and harmony. But peace and harmony will never be established through congresses. Peace and harmony, and conditions worthy of humanity, can only be established when it is the gods who speak to us. When will the gods speak to us?

We had better first ask: When do human beings speak to us? They speak to us when they have a larynx. Human beings would not be able to speak to us without a larynx.

What the gods of nature have given us in our larynx we can pass on to the whole of the world when we find appropriate artistic forms, and through these forms the gods will speak to us. We only need to understand how we can enter into this great process.[6]

Colour in buildings

It seems fitting today that we should speak of something that concerns us very closely, namely, this home of ours for anthroposophical work in Stuttgart. Perhaps for all of you who have entered this hall, and then with a kind of inner vision try to survey the feelings which come over you here, there is a word which may describe what we should like to indicate as the special characteristic of our experience today, namely, mood, feeling, atmosphere;[7] we have doubtless a special feeling, a special frame of mind when we are gathered together in this room. If one follows this feeling further through spiritual perception one may from this standpoint look into the very foundations of our life.

The most noticeable thing is, that we are surrounded by a certain shade of colour which has been used for this room [*a deep ultramarine*]. The fact that in many respects combinations of colour play a great part with us you will also have seen from the way in which we have tried to present the Mystery Plays, and also from the colours of other rooms which we have been able to dedicate to our work.

Aspects of a New Architecture 141

Colour appropriate for an activity

Now it is by no means a matter of indifference to a person in a certain frame of mind what kind of colour surrounds him. And further, it is not immaterial what principal shade of colour acts upon a person of this or that temperament, intellectual nature or character. It is also not immaterial for the whole organization of the human being whether a certain shade of colour acts upon us by being repeated again and again for a long time, or whether it acts only temporarily. You will remember that we decorated the hall that served us for the 1907 Congress with a certain shade of red; but from this the conclusion must not be drawn that red is always the right colour for a lecture room. The room here we have decorated in a different colour. And if anyone asks the reason for these different procedures, the answer is that the hall at Munich was used only for a few days for a particular festive occasion, an event which was over in a few days, and was intended to rouse the frame of mind appropriate to that occasion. But here we have a workroom in which our Stuttgart friends will do their anthroposophical work and carry on their studies from week to week. Essentially we are dealing with a room that will be used for regular lectures.

Colour as an activity of spiritual beings

You will best realize the significance of colour if we describe how it affects the spiritual scientist. For this it is necessary that a person should free himself completely from everything else and devote himself to a particular colour, immerse himself in it. If the person who devotes himself to the colour which covers these physically dense walls were one who had made certain occult progress, it would come about that after a period of this complete devotion the walls themselves would disappear from his clairvoyant vision; awareness that the walls shut off the outer world would vanish. What appears first of all instead is not merely that he sees the neighbouring houses outside, that the walls become like glass, but that into the sphere which opens up there enters a world of purely spiritual phenomena; spiritual facts and spiritual beings become visible. We need only reflect that behind everything around us physically there are spiritual beings and facts. What underlies physical objects outside us in a certain way becomes visible, but what becomes visible is not the same if there are different surroundings. The worlds that surround us spiritually are of many kinds; many different kinds of elemental beings are around us.[8] These elemental beings are not enclosed in boxes, nor in such a state that they live in various fixed dwellings. The law of impenetrability only applies to the physical world, while interpenetrability is the law for the higher worlds. But these beings cannot all be seen in the same way; according to the capacity of clairvoyant vision there may be visible and invisible beings in the same space.

The different spiritual beings behind different colours

What spiritual beings become visible in any particular instance depends upon the colour to which we devote ourselves. In a red room other beings become visible than in a blue room, when one penetrates to them by means of colour. We may now ask: What happens if one is not clairvoyant? What the clairvoyant does consciously is still done unconsciously by the etheric body of a person who is not clairvoyantly trained; this still enters into a certain relation with these same beings. The consequence of this is nothing less than that, according to our surroundings, we come in contact with one or another kind of spiritual being. Now, further, it is a case of being able to establish a favourable or unfavourable connection with the beings that surround us. Let us suppose that we use a colour for the room that brings us into connection with beings who disturb us in what we do in this room; then the colour is unfavourable. Conversely, our etheric body may be assisted by spiritual beings through using the corresponding colour; this is then of course favourable. Now this room here is devoted to repeated study through which we desire to progress in our knowledge. If we have to work in such a room as this it is necessary that we should be able fully to devote ourselves with our entire human organization to what is presented here. We do not wish to be disturbed by anything; we wish to work under the best conditions so that we may absorb these things as well as possible. Naturally one person will absorb them better, another not so well, but the best possible conditions should be created, so that each one can devote himself—to the extent that his own inner capacities allow—to studies that are here presented. The colour surrounding us here brings us in touch with beings in our spiritual environment who come to help us in our etheric body in the spiritual activities that we need in order to approach spiritual truths within us. In such a building and such a room as this we are least disturbed; our etheric body is not burdened by combating prejudicial influences from certain elementary beings, but is able to work more easily.

Red as a colour for festivals

Thus we see that for work that is continually repeated, and for which there must be a certain calmness of soul as a foundation, this precise type of surrounding must be chosen. But then let us suppose that we have to deal with something particularly earnest, but of temporary duration. In this case, if we consider occult laws, it is very advantageous—not only for a festive spirit but also for inward strength—to surround ourselves with red. If we have to make strong will decisions we must overcome the spiritual beings who interfere with this. That is to say, on festive occasions we must become strong, so that what we receive may become a permanent impulse; and unsympathetic feelings on such an occasion would simply mean that one refuses to master weaknesses of disposition and does not allow earnest decisions of the will to be made which, although roused in a short time, are to remain permanently. The effects of colour are extremely important.

The blue sky as an image of the cosmos

Now you know that under certain circumstances in our general environment we see a fundamental colour outspread above us — the blue of the sky. This blue of the sky is very important to the people of our times, for through the blue expanse of space working upon their souls they are continually called upon to come into touch with beings in the cosmos who act upon us through this colour, and who summon our etheric body to turn towards the spiritual. This effect of the blue sky on human beings was not always as it is now. People of the present day think that human beings have always been as they are now, but the entire constitution of the human being has changed in the course of time. In ancient days, when human beings possessed an original clairvoyance, there was no blue sky such as exists for present humanity. At that time, when people gazed out into the expanse above them, their vision was not limited by the blue sky. Instead they saw into the spiritual worlds which lie out there in what we call 'space'. When our ancient ancestors spoke of heaven beginning there, above them, and that the spiritual beings of the hierarchies are to be found there, they expressed the literal truth.[9]

Coloured windows

Those colours which appear transparent [*the coloured windows in the room*] are again different from the colour on a wall, through which we cannot see. When we observe this shining, translucent colour we have to say: Just as through the colour on the opaque walls we enter into relation with certain beings, so through the transparent shining colours [*of the windows*] we enter into relation with other beings. While the beings with whom we come in touch through the opaque walls are primarily spread through space but really have nothing to do with the three kingdoms below us, the mineral, plant and animal kingdoms, through translucent colours we come into contact with the beings directly occupied with bringing into being the manifestations of the three kingdoms of nature. When we look particularly through shining red we come in touch with particular kinds of beings within the kingdoms of nature. When shining red forms a kind of window through which to look clairvoyantly into the kingdoms of nature we meet with beings whose work forms the best forces for the future of our earth existence.[10] They have to be there in the kingdoms of nature so that inner forces may develop in human beings that make them more and more chaste in their blood, that is to say, in their life of passion.

And when we look into the kingdoms of nature in this way we are looking upon those beings which, although we may not be aware of it, urge us most powerfully to purify our passions.[11]

8. Rudolf Steiner on the First Goetheanum

Rudolf Steiner with a model of the first Goetheanum

The following is an edited version of an illustrated talk Steiner gave in The Hague in February 1921. It is one of a number of slide shows in which he talked people through the building.

He begins by describing the function of the building as giving artistic expression to the truths about the human being revealed by spiritual science. Like any other serious work of modern architecture, it is a question of form being an outcome of function. In Steiner's case, however, one could say that he has extended the concept of functionalism to include 'spiritual function'. Once again he talks about the ability of art to express the truths of spiritual science in another medium.

He then goes on to talk about the forces inherent in nature as the basis of his inspiration, not in the sense of imitation but '. . . to steep myself in nature's creation of organic forms and from these to obtain organic forms which, when metamorphosed, might make a single whole of the Dornach building – that is, organic forms that are of such a kind that each single form must be in the place where it is.' Steiner illustrates this point with examples of details such as a column supporting the main staircase and a radiator cover.

The talk includes a discussion of the seven 'planetary' columns in the larger dome. On this occasion he discusses the respective mirroring of forms either side of the fourth, central motif (1–7, 2–6 and 3–5). It is interesting to compare this account with the description given in 1907, reproduced in chapter 6, in which he concentrates on the metamorphosis of one form into the next.

The talk also includes some discussion of the paintings on the ceilings and how they relate to the coloured background. The paintings themselves are a subject in their own right but I have included comments Steiner made here about the central motif at the rear of the small dome and the sculpture that was intended to stand beneath it as the focal point of the interior. This depicts the figure of Christ as the archetype of the human being, holding the balance between the gravitational force of Ahriman beneath him and the weight-defying influence of Lucifer above.[1] This sculpture is, simultaneously, a representation of the basic forces at work in the human body and architecture, as we saw in chapter 1, and also a picture of the human condition. These two forces work into us in manifold ways, too numerous and complex to outline further in this book, for example: expansion and contraction; light and dark; heat and cold – all of which have both a physical aspect and a soul equivalent.[2]

I have said that the style of this Goetheanum has arisen out of the same sources that gave birth to spiritual science. The endeavour to create a new style of architecture is accompanied by inevitable risks, by all the imperfections which must accompany such a first attempt. In reality it is out of the springs of being, not out of thought or mere experimental and mentally interpreted investigations, that anthroposophy itself arises out of the very fount of existence. Therefore in all that it creates it must be united with the creative forces which, for example, are active in nature herself. For the ultimate creative forces in nature, as I have explained in preceding lectures, are indeed of a spiritual character themselves. Let me use a metaphor here. Take a nut for instance. It contains a kernel, and this kernel is formed according to definite principles. But there is also the shell of the nut, and this could not be otherwise than it is, given the nut's intrinsic nature. The same force that forms the kernel also forms the nutshell. The shell, then, is formed according to the laws of nature just as much as is the kernel. In Dornach, anthroposophical spiritual science will be taught from the stage.[3] The content of anthroposophical spiritual science will be examined and studied. Artistic performances will be given—truly artistic ones, not merely symbolic or full of empty allegory, but performances that are an outward expression of the same thing of which spiritual science is itself an expression. Around all this therefore—we may say, around the kernel of the nut—there must also be formed a shell that is shaped exactly according to the same laws.

In Dornach, then, a kind of architecture has been cultivated that has the same meaning and the same spirit as anthroposophical spiritual science itself. The sculpture within the building will express the same spirit, as will the painting there. Whoever stands at the rostrum and there expresses himself in ideas will only be expressing in another way what speaks to us from the columns, from the paintings on the walls, and from the sculpted forms. It is all—if I may use a somewhat trivial expression—from one mould!

People are so very fearful that nothing really artistic can be produced in this way, but only something symbolic or allegoric. But ladies and gentlemen, in Dornach there is not a single symbol, not a single allegory, but rather we have attempted to give everything truly artistic form. Nor will the ideas that are expressed be in any way embodied in pictures. That would be inartistic. The common spiritual life that underlies it all can at one moment be given shape in art, at another in ideas—that is to say in thoughts, using a scientific approach. Nor again is the art in Dornach a didactic expression, as it were, of science. Rather it may be said to be one mode of representation, and science another, of the same great spiritual mystery from which, in anthroposophical spiritual science, everything is drawn which the latter strives to give to humanity.

The whole outer form of the Dornach building had to be in keeping with these ideas. Anyone looking at this Dornach building will see a double-domed structure. Side by side stand two cylinder-like structures which, however, intersect each other; and above these, two hemispherical domes which are bound together in a circular segment by means of a somewhat difficult mechanical contrivance.

Since in Dornach the things that can be investigated through spiritual science are to be brought forth into the world, this must also be expressed in the building itself. The part under the small dome is a kind of stage. Here there will be presented Mystery Plays[4] and the like. Eurythmy[5] will also be performed and there are plans for many other things. The lecturer's desk stands between the small and the large dome. Under the larger dome is the auditorium, seating about a thousand people. In this double-domed building is expressed the fact that anthroposophical spiritual science has things to impart to present and future humanity, in relation to spiritual, human and social matters, which I discussed in the two preceding lectures.

When one approaches the building from the west and comes to the main entrance facing west, one is met by the following view. The foundation of the building is concrete. Above this is a terrace surrounding the greater part of the building. Upon this concrete foundational structure stands a structure of wood. The domes are covered with that wonderful northern slate, gleaming in the sunlight, which is to be found in the slate quarries you can see when travelling between Christiania [*now Oslo*] and Bergen. It came from the Voss slate quarries. This slate blends in a marvellous fashion with the building's architectural conception.

Concrete and wood are both employed to give rise to an architectural style that may perhaps be described as the transition from previous geometrical, symmetrical, mechanical, static-dynamic architectural styles into an organic style. Not that some sort of organic form has been imitated in the Dornach building. That is not the case.

Rather it has been my aim, in accordance with Goethe's theory of metamorphosis, to steep myself in nature's creation of organic forms, and from these to obtain organic forms that, when metamorphosed, might make a single whole of the Dornach building. In other words, organic forms of such a kind that each single form must be in precisely the place it is.

Let us think for a moment of the nature of organic forms. Think of something apparently quite insignificant in the organic form of the human organism — the lobe of the ear. We cannot help realizing that this ear lobe, in the place where it is, could not be different since the whole organism is as we see it. The least and the greatest in an organic whole has its place in the organism, its absolutely right form. All this has passed over into the architectural conception of the Dornach building.

I well know how much may be said against this organic principle of building from the point of view of older architectural styles. This organic style, however, has been attempted in the architectural conception of the building at Dornach. Old perspectives may of course reject this — but they have, after all, always rejected everything new. But at all events, if one can be reconciled to this transition from static-dynamic and geometrical architectural forms into organic forms, it will be found that such transition is experienced in conformity with the same inner laws by which the leaf of a plant at the lower part of the stem, let us say, is metamorphosed when it appears higher up on the stem (though it is not a matter of naturalistic imitation). It

Rudolf Steiner on the First Goetheanum 155

is always the same form, yet transformed in manifold ways.

You will therefore find in the Dornach building certain organic forms such as you see here, carved out of wood, as embodied in the capitals of the columns at the entrance. Here in the window at the side you see the same motif, apparently no longer the same, yet only metamorphosed, just as in the petals of a flower the motif of the green leaf of a plant reappears.

If one looks at the building both from the inside and from the outside, one has the impression that whatever motif appears in the design around the entrance is developed differently there than elsewhere. We see, therefore, as we approach the entrance, that here it has less weight to carry, whereas in that part where the whole weight of the building lies it must respond to this weight.

Throughout the whole architectural conception of the building we have paid attention to everything that may be found in nature in the development of the forms of bones and muscles. If you consider the bone structure within the knee, the wonderful inspiration of nature has so shaped certain bones that they constitute the basic structure and support what rests upon them. Their forms expand or contract in the right places. This inner feeling for the shapes of organic formative process, for the shapes that are to carry weight—this was essential in order to construct the Dornach building.

Here you see a remarkable structure. This is what is subject to the most severe criticism from some quarters. This [*boiler-house*] structure stands close to the building. I proceeded from the conception that lighting and heating installations were like the kernel of a nut, and I undertook to create for these a shell of concrete—a material which it

Rudolf Steiner on the First Goetheanum 157

The building viewed from a point on the north side

is extremely difficult to mould artistically. Those who criticize this structure today do not pause to reflect what would stand there if no endeavour had been made to mould something artistic out of concrete—a material so difficult to mould. There could be nothing but a brick chimney. I wonder whether that would be more beautiful than this, which is of course only a first attempt to give a certain style to something made of concrete. It has many defects, for it is only a first attempt to mould something artistic out of materials such as concrete.

Here you see seven columns on each side of the larger dome. Here, in the curve of the small dome, six columns. There are not seven because of any mystical significance, but simply from artistic considerations. As the violin has

158 Architecture

Rudolf Steiner's model, looking from the small dome into the larger dome

four strings, so here artistic feelings, springing from inner reasons, have shown that a certain artistic evolution would be achieved, and also an artistic conclusion, if exactly seven motifs were to be developed. In these columns we have tried to shape the motifs of the capitals and architraves not as repetitions but as a living development. As we enter through the west door, we encounter the first two columns. These two are alike. When however we proceed from the first to the second column, the capital of the second column, as well as its base and the architrave above it, is shaped in accordance with an organic necessity. Its shape is such that it was necessary to enter livingly into the creative and shaping process of the forces of nature in order to develop this motif of the second column from that of the first, of the third from the second, until a definite conclusion had been reached in the motif of the seventh. Many visitors who come to Dornach ask: 'What does each capital mean?' This is something one can never ask about a work of art. The essential thing is that artistically and structurally one column grows out of another, whereas in the static style of architecture one only really considers symmetry, with [*unchanging*] repetitions of the same motif. Here one has to do with a living evolution from the first to the seventh column. So I shall show you these columns later on, and then you will be able to understand this.

First of all I had to work out the entire building as a model, so that even the structural scheme of the building, the ground-plan and elevation which were then actually

Original model, cross-sectioned vertically through the centre

used, were formed according to this model. The whole, indeed, embodies the Dornach architectural conception. It is real experience, in the same way as spiritual science itself. It is in a certain sense another expression of what spiritual science itself expresses.

Here you see part of the building adjoining the main entrance and containing the stairway to the auditorium, also a house close by. This house has a special history. The building itself [*the Goetheanum*] was made possible by the sympathy and help of one of our friends in the anthroposophical movement. The fact that the Dornach hill has become the site of our building is due to a friend in Basle, who long ago bought this site for a summer house for

West entrance with Duldeck house in the background

himself. He then gave this land to us, and so we were able to erect our building. This friend also wished to have his own house here. So it became my task—and this for various reasons—to design a house with about 15 rooms, to be built of concrete. This was certainly a new departure. There are indeed defects in this house, which has been built artistically out of concrete. But one has to make a beginning with these things.

A side wing (south entrance)

These two side wings are fitted in like a cross-beam. Here the principal motif is again metamorphosed. Everywhere the same and yet always something different is contained, as it were, in the forms of this building.

Here again in the side wing the design, which in the

case of the front entrance is elaborate and worked out in a rich mass of material, is more simply developed in the same metamorphosis. Everywhere a certain principle of symmetry is maintained, but linked with artistic asymmetry. This asymmetry makes the building artistically satisfying, and creates a great deal of variation.

Then you see here a column that supports the stairway [*see page 166*].

The motif of the stairs themselves is so worked out that it moves organically upwards into the heart of the building to the right and descends to the left towards the entrance. The stairs here are borne up by a column that does not imitate an organic motif in some naturalistic fashion, but has an organic shape in the same way that the forms of living beings in nature are shaped by nature's creative forces. The way in which the top of this column rises up on the side gives support to something so that it can more easily be carried. And the way in which it braces itself on the right-hand side where the main weight of the building rests is brought to expression in the smallest detail, just as in the form of the ear lobe a unity with the whole human organism is expressed. Every form in Dornach must be felt as a necessity in its place.

Here is a motif which I have carried out in the most varied metamorphoses. In this place it is moulded out of concrete, while in the upper part of this wing it is formed of wood. It is a form that stands in front of a radiator [*See page 167*]. As I have said, things have been done in Dornach in a way that enables individual forms to grow

164 ARCHITECTURE

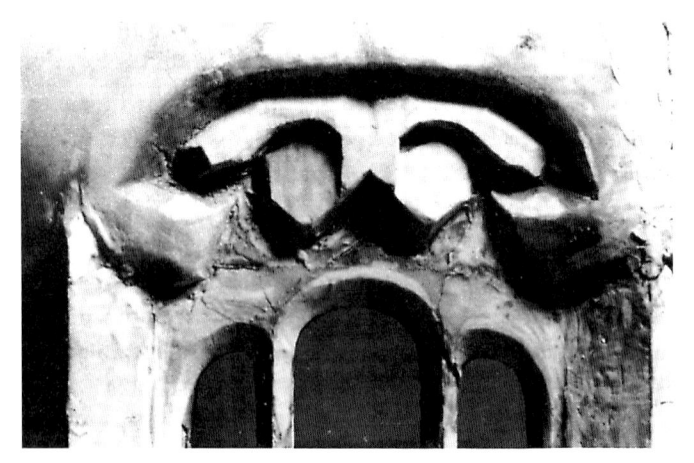

Three of Steiner's working models, with variations on the principal motif

Rudolf Steiner on the First Goetheanum 165

out of one another through metamorphosis. One does not in some abstract fashion have merely architectural forms suitable for a utilitarian kind of building, but everything is carried out in a thoroughly artistic and organic way.

The seven columns and architraves

One capital really develops out of another; it is not 'thought out' but one feels it like a leaf on the stem of a plant out of which others proceed in a metamorphosed form. So here too the following motif is always shaped out of the preceding one purely through laws of artistic feeling.

Column supporting main stairway (see page 163)

It thus became clear to me that we can only rightly understand the nature of evolution if we perceive this artistic method of working. We generally imagine that in evolutionary progression earlier forms are the simplest and that then they become more and more complicated. But this is not the case. If we work artistically, allowing

Rudolf Steiner on the First Goetheanum

A radiator cover

one form really to develop out of the other, we find that the simpler shapes itself into the more complicated, it is true; yet when the complexity has reached a certain definite point, harmony and greater simplicity arise once again.

The process of evolution is as follows: from the simple to the complex—and then again to simplification. This is surprising at first. We form something in this way out of pure artistic feeling and then find that it corresponds with the artistic creations of nature. The human eye is the most

168 Architecture

The seven columns and architraves in the larger dome (Steiner's model). The sequence as shown here is from right to left on the south side of the space

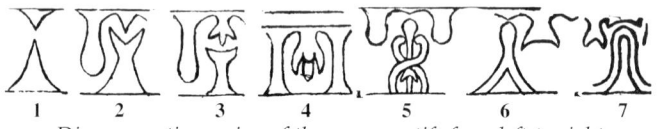

Diagrammatic version of the seven motifs from left to right (based on Steiner's sketches)

perfect of all organs, but not the most complex. Certain organs belonging to the lower animals are omitted in the case of the human eye. We arrive at this spontaneously when we form things in a purely artistic way. I hit upon something very remarkable in this connection. I said to myself that I must have seven columns, but not, I assure you, because of any 'mystical' considerations. The seventh column simply stood there as the conclusion. One could not proceed any further; the motifs had reached their end. Later on, however, I discovered that when I started on the convex form of the seventh column and shaped something artistic, the convex motif fitted into the concave form of the first column. I did not set out to do this. It was exactly the same with the sixth and the second columns, and also with the fifth and the third. I discovered this both in the case of the capitals and the bases. It was not sought for but arose from the approach I adopted. We find in nature herself such surprising connections between forms. Thus

Fourth and fifth capitals ('Mars' and 'Mercury', from right to left). Note that the Mercury motif appears over the 'Mars' column before descending and becoming a capital.

when we are creating artistically we find such connections in the individual forms that arise. We arrive at a deeper understanding first of nature's mysterious weaving and working, and then of the world of form itself, into which man can penetrate through artistic imagination and perception.

One column alone has become relatively more complex. You will see, however, that this motif, as it develops from above downwards and from below upwards, gives rise to something that I did not try to obtain. Yet when people look at it they will say: He has sculpted the caduceus of Mercury (or Mercury staff). I did not have the deliberate intention of forming this, but this is how it came about.

Painting in the Goetheanum

Now here is another view from the auditorium, the last two columns of which you see here, looking towards the stage. This shows the interior of the stage [*smaller*] dome with its paintings. As for the painting of the two domes, I am unable to show you very distinct pictures. In the smaller dome, at any rate, a serious endeavour was made to pursue the real nature of a new art of painting. Everything created through painting must flow out of colour itself. The world of colour is a world in itself. If we really understand the world of colour we know the creative quality of each individual colour. There is a creative element underlying the harmony of colour. Those who

Rudolf Steiner on the First Goetheanum 171

View through the proscenium opening looking into the smaller dome

know how red expresses itself from within, who know how blue works, grow to be able to shape the world of painting out of the realm of colour.

This was the attempt made in the painting of the small dome in Dornach. The essential thing is the colour in each part of it. Figures arise there from the colour, but everything originally developed out of colour itself. It is really only light, shade and colour that are able to express anything on a flat surface. The outline element of drawing is always contrary to truth. Let us take the horizontal line: above, the blue sky; below, the greenish sea. Paint it in this way and the horizon appears as the creation of the colour boundaries themselves. It is the same with every line in painting. In painting, form is the work of colour—and it is this we have attempted to realize in Dornach.

Here now you see what is painted in the middle—a representative of humanity. Each one who sees this representative of humanity may feel it to be an embodiment of the figure of Christ. This figure of Christ, which is there in the centre, is formed in accordance with my—as I think—supersensible vision of the figure of Christ as he really lived in Palestine at the beginning of our era. The traditional figure of Christ, with the beard, was only invented in the fifth or sixth century. We have to go back, by means of spiritual-scientific investigation, to the time when Christ lived in Palestine in order to find his form through supersensible vision. I do not ask people to believe on my authority that this is the true figure of

Rudolf Steiner on the First Goetheanum

Painting of the 'Representative of Humanity'

Christ. But I see it thus, and my inmost being tells me that this is the figure of Christ.

Below, worked into a rock, is the figure of Ahriman. From the right arm of Christ proceed flashes of lightning which wind round the ahrimanic figure like serpents. The ahrimanic figure is all that man would be if he possessed intellect alone, and had only a materialistic frame of mind, without heart. Above is the figure of Lucifer, in red — everything in man that inclines towards fantasy, one-sided theosophy, mysticism, etc. Here you see this figure of Lucifer, the face painted entirely in red, above the figure of Christ. The wings of the Ahriman figure are batlike, firmly held fast by the flashes proceeding from the hand of Christ.

Of course, the essential thing is to feel all this out of the colour itself. All this is what you see painted at the extreme eastern section of the small cupola. Below this painting of Christ, Lucifer and Ahriman is a group carved in wood, 31 feet high, in the centre of which you again find the representative of humanity, of whom one may have the feeling that it is Christ.

Above this representative of humanity, in two forms, is the Lucifer motif; below it, again in two forms, the Ahriman motif. Then up above, appearing out of the rock, an elemental being who, in the manner of a nature being, is looking at Christ between Lucifer and Ahriman.

I have ventured to form a face quite asymmetrically so that it arises naturally out of the composition of the group. A composition is usually such that it is made up of several figures. Here in this group, each separate figure is always

Rudolf Steiner on the First Goetheanum   175

Central part of the 'Group' sculpture, showing the central figure and one each of the forms depicting Lucifer and Ahriman

The nature being with its asymmetrical face, seen above one of the two Lucifer forms (full-size plasticine model by Steiner)

fashioned out of the sense and spirit of the whole composition. Hence this asymmetrical form. It is a face that is quite asymmetrical, but it has to be like this because of its position relative to the other figures in the group.

The boiler-house

And now, standing by itself, you see the separate building that provides heat and light. Here you see it from the rear. Its form is wholly suitable to the machinery it contains.

Rudolf Steiner working on the central figure of the 'Group' sculpture

178 Architecture

The boiler-house, 1914, from the rear with the second Goetheanum in the background

Rudolf Steiner on the First Goetheanum 179

The whole is incomplete unless smoke comes out there, up above. When this occurs you will have the feeling that these shapes are also justified. [*See chapter 6*]

In art one creates out of form and cannot give an abstract explanation why it is like this or that. Some people think the forms look like leaves or ears. But this is not the point; the chief thing is the form which is adapted, on the one hand, to the position of the boiler-house; and on the other hand to what takes place within it, its function.

The glass studio

This is the glass studio where the glass windows were carved. These windows were then put into the auditorium of the Goetheanum. They are carved out of large sheets of thick glass tinged with a single colour. There is quite a long story connected with this! First of all we had ordered sheets of glass from a factory near Paris. These went such a roundabout way and took so long to arrive that they disappeared on the battlefield. We never saw anything of them. We had to order the glass a second time. The idea is that with the aid of special instruments a design is cut engraved into a large, single-coloured pane of glass. Then the window is put in, and only when sunlight passes through does the work of art appear. This is connected with the whole idea of the Dornach building. Everywhere else we find buildings with walls that set limits to a certain space. In Dornach we are concerned with walls that do not suggest the idea that you are cut off from the outside. All that I have just shown you makes the walls transparent, artistically speaking. While in the building, the observer or member of the audience has the feeling that the walls surrounding him are permeable and transparent, artistically transparent, and that he is connected through them with the whole universe.

This is expressed physically in an artistic way by means of these glass windows which as etchings in glass are only something like the score of music from which the musician plays. They only become a work of art when the sunlight plays through them. Thus what is in the building extends itself into the sun-filled world of nature outside.

Rudolf Steiner on the First Goetheanum   181

An impression of coloured shadows in the first Goetheanum, by Wilfred Nerton (original picture in colour)

Grinding of the glass had to be done in this studio, which now serves as the Goetheanum administrative office.

The panes of glass are not all of the same colour. Panes of different colours are used so that when we enter the building we see before us a harmonious interplay of many colours from the various windows. The whole of the space is then shone through by a symphony of colour which, when sensed artistically, is composed of the most varied shades.

Now, ladies and gentlemen, I have taken the liberty of presenting to you in a number of pictures the idea and conception of the building at Dornach. I have also explained how this idea aims to establish an organic style of building in place of the merely static, geometrical style. This had to take place because the spiritual science I present in lectures is not a narrow science but full of life, since it aims to draw fully from the fount of life of the universe itself and of humanity.

Hence it is not merely a phrase when we speak of uniting religion, science and social conditions. Simply out of the entire nature of spiritual science, the building with its new style had to express what spiritual science itself expresses in thoughts or laws.

The sacrifice and generosity of a large number of friends has enabled us to proceed so far with the building that last autumn about 30 people, representing various professions, were able to give several series of lectures there; and at Easter, again, a shorter series of lectures will be held. But the building is not nearly finished. We may only express the hope that we shall be able to finish this building, as the centre from which should proceed a spiritual-scientific movement that can bring about the social emancipation necessary for people of the present day and also of the near future.

With regard to the building at Dornach I know perfectly well that many objections to it can be raised from points of view that adhere to the past and to old styles of architecture. But if one were never to venture something new, the evolution of humanity could never progress. And, above all, what proceeds from Dornach as anthroposophy is concerned with this impulse towards progress, through the evolution of humanity towards the goals I indicated at the end of yesterday's lecture.

9. The Second Goetheanum Building

The first Goetheanum building was destroyed by arson during the night between 31 December 1922 and 1 January 1923. Some ten years of pioneering work were lost in one night. This was a devastating blow given the central importance Steiner attached to art and architecture in enabling humanity to experience spiritual phenomena through the senses in a more direct and immediate way than is possible through thinking or meditation.

But precisely because of what was at stake, Steiner immediately set to work on the concept for a new building.

There is some evidence that the first building would have been built in concrete if Steiner's collaborators had not wanted to use wood. Steiner normally deferred to people's wishes when it came to putting spiritual science into practice, but the second time round he decided he needed to take complete control, perhaps because he felt there was too much at stake.

Much can be said about the radical change in form language in this second building. One obvious point, which Steiner makes himself in the following article, is the building as a response to the limestone hills of the Swiss Jura which rise above the site to the east. The first building did not make a satisfactory relationship with its environment and surrounding landscape.[1] Furthermore, the principle aspect of the building was its interior space, as we have seen from earlier chapters. It was a modern mystery centre in which 'the gods could speak' to humanity.

With the second building Steiner concentrated on its exterior form. The entire building was turned inside out so that the seven columns which appeared inside on each side of the larger dome in the first building were transformed into vertical elements on the north and south facades of the second building. This in itself was a metamorphic transformation. There is also another dynamic form of metamorphosis in the development of the primary cubic form of the building. The cubic form of the stage on the east side develops into the trapezoid form of the main auditorium, as can be seen from the ground plan (see below). Besides this, however, the entire building also becomes progressively more dynamic as the form is developed sculpturally from east to west.

186 ARCHITECTURE

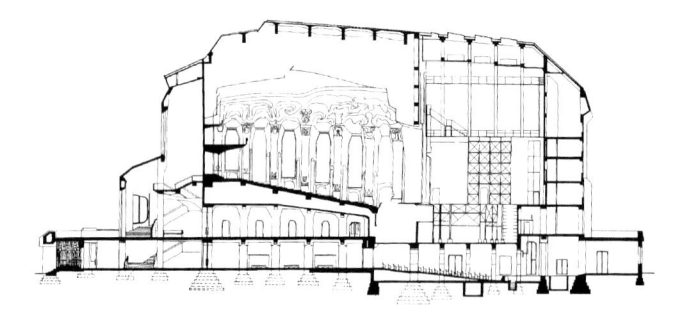

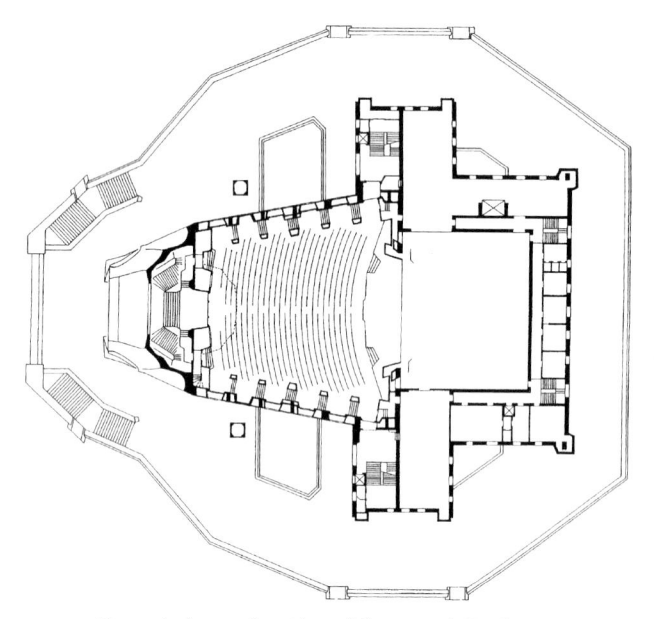

Ground plan and section of the second Goetheanum

The reasons for turning the building inside out are connected with a complete transformation of the social form in which spiritual science, or anthroposophy, had been practised up to that time.[2] The building is an artistic representation of this social metamorphosis. If the first building enclosed an interior where the 'gods spoke' to the human being in a protected inner space, the space addressed by the second building is, in effect, the entire earth. This expresses, I think, a supremely Christian thought on Steiner's part – the realization that, since the Mystery of Golgotha, as he called it, the earth itself has become a temple.

The following article was published in a local newspaper and is reproduced here with the editor's foreword.

Article in *Die National-Zeitung* newspaper, Basle, 1 November 1924

The rebuilding of the Goetheanum has given rise to considerable discussion in the press and aroused interest in the widest circles. We are now in a position to publish a picture of the future building and we have also invited Dr Rudolf Steiner to expound on the concept of the building. (Newspaper editor.)

The proposed rebuilding has posed no easy task for giving expression to its architectural conception. A total reorientation was necessary since the old building was constructed essentially in wood while the new one is to be built entirely in concrete. In addition, the design had to be compatible with the essence of the anthroposophy which is to be cultivated within its walls. Anthroposophy draws on spiritual sources from which flow both the knowledge of the spirit and also, for those sensitive to it, the shapes and forms of artistic style. It seeks the primordial forces of knowledge, which are also the very origins of artistic form and design. Thus it would be grotesque if anthroposophy's own building were to be designed by someone with quite different aesthetic sentiments and with only a superficial feeling for the essence of anthroposophy. This place of work can only be designed by someone for whom the experience of every detail comes from the same spiritual vision as does the knowledge contained in every word spoken out of anthroposophy.

Organic forms in the old wooden Goetheanum

Because of the softness of wood it was possible to shape space in conformity with the way nature shapes organic forms. An organism as a whole creates for even its smallest parts—an ear lobe, for example—a shape that cannot be other than it is. By entering artistically into the way nature creates organic forms and raising this through creative imagination to a spiritual level it was possible to create an 'organic style of architecture' as opposed to one based merely on static or dynamic forces. Thus there was in the old Goetheanum a vestibule which visitors entered before going into the main auditorium. The forms carved in the wood indicated quite clearly that it was a space to receive people coming in from outside. Another factor that determined the way the wood was shaped was the need for everything to fit organically with the building as a whole. From this, in turn, arose the exterior design, which revealed artistically how the building was both formed and articulated to meet the requirements of the anthroposophical work taking place within it.

The convex character of the new concrete building

The architectural conception now has to be handled quite differently since it is a question of using concrete rather than wood. For this reason it took nearly a year before the new design model could be made. With wood, the shape of the space is carved into the material; a form arises from a concave hollowing of the surface. With concrete, on the other hand, the form is convex, a bulging-out of the surface defining the boundary of the space required. This also shows in the way the exterior forms come about. Surfaces, lines and angles all have to be handled according to the way the forms and shapes on the inside press outwards into them, making themselves visible.

In addition to all this we shall have to work more economically with space in this second Goetheanum than was the case in the first. This first building basically consisted of a single space that was able to provide artistic surroundings for both lectures and performances. There will now be two levels, the lower one comprising offices, lecture rooms and a rehearsal stage, and the upper one the auditorium and main stage, which can also be used for lectures.

Architectural design responds to practical necessities

Artistic shaping of the exterior lines and surfaces had to evolve from this interior design. The way the roof is shaped is a case in point—it will not be domed this time. Those who respond sensitively to the architectural forms will sense our attempt at an artistic solution that follows the rise of the auditorium at the front, and at the rear follows the enclosing walls of the stage with its storage rooms. Unbiased artistic appraisal may reveal how the underlying necessities in the design of the plan have been followed through in the whole architectural concept, including the daring execution of the western facade.

The building is to stand on a terrace, which will enable people to walk round the building at a level higher than ground level. Wide, sweeping stairs will lead up from ground level to the entrances on the terrace. Cloakrooms and other facilities will be located beneath the terrace.

The design and its setting in the landscape

The author of this architectural concept is convinced that the shape of this concrete building will be in complete

The Second Goetheanum Building

harmony with the group of surrounding hills on which the Goetheanum is fortunate to stand. When creating the wooden structure of the earlier building the architect was not yet as familiar with their shapes as he is now, having come to know and love them during the course of more than a decade. The spirit of the surrounding countryside has therefore also been incorporated into the building in a way not possible eleven years ago.

The second Goetheanum with the Jura mountains in the background

10. The Architecture of a Community in Dornach

The following lecture was a response to the desire of a number of anthroposophists to settle in Dornach and build houses around the Goetheanum building. The building and surrounding land was to become the centre of the anthroposophical movement, and Steiner had moved there himself. In this lecture he is treading a line between the freedom of individuals to build what they like and the need to create an architectural unity in what was to become a campus. In the event, a number of the new inhabitants asked Steiner to design their houses, starting with the Duldeck house which he refers to in chapter 8. Altogether Steiner designed eight houses and five other buildings on or near the Goetheanum site between 1914 and 1924.

Freedom of initiative, a prerequisite

Now that the construction of the Goetheanum is under way at Dornach, a number of our members are hoping to set up home nearby, and some have already enquired about sites, with the intention of building private houses in which to live all the year round, or at least for part of the year. What I now want to say in this connection should not, of course, be interpreted as a wish on my part to

The Architecture of a Community in Dornach 193

interfere in any way with what people intend to undertake in the vicinity of the Goetheanum. It should be clearly understood, in keeping with the way we interpret our anthroposophical movement, that the freedom of each individual member must be respected to the utmost. Thus it is not my intention even to hint at any sort of compulsion. I may, however, be permitted to express what would be desirable.

In the first place we shall have, at Dornach, the Goetheanum itself. We have tried to find a way of building originating in a truly new approach that can express, in architectural forms, what we are aiming at. So at long last we may create something that will represent not only a dignified but also an appropriate home for our work.

Dr Grosheintz has shown you illustrations that demonstrate the efforts that have already been made to achieve this goal. If the funds prove adequate, other buildings will, as you have just seen, arise in the immediate vicinity of the Goetheanum. The attempt will be made to carry these out so that they represent an artistic unity with the plans for the Goetheanum itself.

A number of factors have to be considered before such a 'whole' can arise. So far we have only been able to put this idea into practice in the case of one little building, which you can see here in the model [*the glass studio*]. Initially this building is to be used for the engraving of the coloured glass windows. It will be large enough also to house Herr Rychter and perhaps one other person.

The glass studio, 1914, with the second Goetheanum in the background

Form follows function

The boiler-house, which has already taken on a fairly definite form, is a second undertaking in this plan. The problem has been to design this large chimney to be both architecturally in keeping with the main Goetheanum building and constructed in reinforced concrete. It would obviously be a monstrosity if it were to resemble those normally put up.

From the small model and the illustrations shown to you by Dr Grosheintz you will see that the attempt has

The boiler-house, 1914
See also illustrations in chapter 6

been made to solve the architectural character of this building. When it is completed, and particularly when the heating plant is in operation — the smoke has been thought of as part of the architecture — it will be possible to feel that this chimney has a beauty of its own. This will be despite its prosaic function, by virtue of the fact that its task is expressed in its shape — even though this shape has not arisen according to utilitarian architecture as conceived hitherto, but as the result of an aesthetic design process.

The two small domes link up with the rest of the structure and the chimney. The rising forms on the latter have been thought to resemble leaves by some or ears by others. But there is no need to define them so long as they are appropriate. The Goetheanum and directly adjacent buildings will be heated from here and the forms will show that a building serving the modern requirements of central heating can at the same time be aesthetically satisfying.

In a task of this sort it is necessary first of all to have exact particulars of the purpose of the proposed building. If you know how many rooms are required and what purpose they are to serve, how many types of vertical communication there are to be, as well as what orientation and outlook the client requires, and if you also know the exact site and how the building is to relate to the Goetheanum, to the north or to the south of it, then I would claim it is possible to find an appropriate architectural solution for every such scheme.

Visual unity of the community

One essential consideration therefore, if we are not to sacrifice our principles, is that it really will be necessary for those friends who want to join the community and build in the neighbourhood of the Goetheanum to make common cause, at least in the wider sense, with what must be attempted in the case of buildings immediately surrounding it. Through the outer appearance, through the whole style of the buildings, it should become apparent to the world at large that all these houses belong together and form a connected whole. Even if other houses are situated among them, it would still be desirable that those put up by members of the anthroposophical community should be so built that one can tell by looking at them that they form part of a greater whole. The outside world may even say, 'What peculiar people.' Let them! What is important is that they can notice this—be it approvingly or disapprovingly. Even if this complex of buildings belonging to the Goetheanum is interspersed with other houses, we want to give cause for people to notice that it comprises an ideal whole.

A home for spiritual science must reveal its essence

A further consideration is that we want to create something that has a real bearing on cultural developments of the present day. From the forms of the Goetheanum itself you can tell that we want our spiritual-scientific approach to enter into architectural style as well as into artistic practice in every field of activity. If asked, for example, about the best way of practising the art of dance we have to seek our own contribution and will come to eurythmy.[1] The same goes for other forms of art. We need to find our own artistic contribution and thus produce something in the world for those who want to understand. Perhaps this

198 Architecture

is only possible for a spiritual stream that is as fruitful as spiritual science.

I have often mentioned an address given by Heinrich Ferstel, architect of the Votivkirche in Vienna and rector of the technical university there. He maintained that architectural styles are not invented. One can argue strongly against this tenet, and one can also prove it to be correct. Both arguments have their logic. Perhaps styles of architecture are indeed not invented, but it does not follow from this contention that one can simply take the Gothic style as Ferstel did and put up the Votivkirche in the form of a somewhat enlarged example of the confectioner's art. Nor does it follow that architectural styles nowadays may only be created out of eclectic combinations and modifications of past styles.

It is precisely the approach to this problem, based on spiritual science, that should show it is possible to infuse architectural design with true art forms born of an inner,

The second Goetheanum from the north, with the boiler-house, glass studio and Eurythmeum

spiritual life. We should prove to the world that this is also possible in the case of private houses. This is an angle that ought to win some understanding for our work, and in showing that we are able to approach such tasks from this point of view we will create meaningful values for the culture of our time.

Cooperation and social endeavour

Hence, although influencing anyone's freedom would be inappropriate, it would indeed be fine if members of the community were, out of their own free will and filled with a recognition of our fundamental principles, to club together to create a homogeneous whole. We have to accept the fact that an existing house, which cannot at the moment be removed, is situated quite near to the Goetheanum and will not exactly enhance the beauty of the site. But although we cannot aim to make everything entirely beautiful, we ought to see to it that what we ourselves do is beautiful in accordance with our understanding.

I cannot help admitting that I have been really depressed recently, after some building plans came to my notice proposing house designs for members of the community. They undoubtedly arose from the best intentions, but they nevertheless exhibited all the monstrosities, all the revolting features of a ghastly style of architecture. Given the requisite good will, there must surely be other

Duldeck House, 1914, from the north-east

ways of doing things. Obviously there will be hindrances and difficulties, but what new venture striving to make its way in the world does not encounter hindrances and difficulties?

Although I do not intend to interfere tomorrow when the members of the community form their association, I nevertheless feel that the prospects will be dim if this leads to anything that goes against what has just been expressed. If we all take the greatest of care, it will be possible to achieve the aim described. But if members of the community lack the patience to wait until a good solution can be found for a given dwelling, then nothing favourable will be able to come about.

The Architecture of a Community in Dornach 201

However easy it may be to understand that some are in a hurry to get their building project under way, it would still be desirable if those who are in earnest about our aims could exercise patience, so that things can be carried out in accordance with intentions that cannot be described as having foundations in our own, personal, will, but which must be called forth through spiritual science. It is quite possible that something may arise that will appear comical in the eyes of the world. Let them laugh! It will stop eventually. If one were never to undertake anything of this kind there would never be any progress in human evolution.

The harmony of outer forms as a reflection of the harmony within the resident community

There is no need to worry that anyone would have to suffer the slightest discomfort in his or her house if the principles I have outlined are adhered to. One thing, however, will be essential, and that is that members of the community do not all go their several ways, but that what gets done is done in harmony; that one can talk things over and rely on one another. The architectural features that will cause the whole community to appear as an ideal unity will be an external imprint of a harmony of an inner kind. I now want to say something that is partly a wish and partly a hypothesis: all the built forms of the community should be an expression of the inner harmony of its inhabitants.

de Jaager House, 1921

So far as the aims of the Anthroposophical Society are concerned, it will be impossible for the faintest trace of discontent or mutual incompatibility or even an unfriendly word to pass from one member of the community to another—let alone any wry glances. It will be wonderful when the very harmony of external forms suffuses everything like a personification of peace and contentment. Forms stimulate thoughts, so even if some should find reason to pull a face or adopt a grim expression, they will regain their contented smile as soon as their eyes alight on these sociable, peaceful forms.

The Architecture of a Community in Dornach   203

Truly organic solutions must be differentiated

All these factors taken together certainly give us reason to strive for a homogeneous result. Do not believe for one moment, however, that the unity will oblige one house to be exactly like another. On the contrary, the houses must be varied and they will have to be very individual in character. Just as there would be nothing organic in putting an arm or hand where the head ought to be in a human body, so a house that would be right for one site would be wrong for another. All this will have to be very carefully thought through for our purposes.

Control of occupation within the community

Apart from setting all this in train, there will still be various other points to take into account. Consider that while we have been gathered here this week, a society of theosophists met in the next room on Monday, and another society on one of the other days. This is all very well. But now imagine that the son or daughter or grandchild of one of our members were to join a different society and then later inherited one of the houses in our community. No longer would we just be sharing premises for lectures in a neighbourly way, for now the different views and attitudes of that society would be present in our very midst.

We must begin now to consider the difficulties that might arise in the course of time, and how such difficulties

Houses for eurythmists, from the north-west. Design by Edith Maryon and Rudolf Steiner, 1920

are to be met. This could only be achieved if an association of members of the community were able to find ways and means to retain the properties of members of the Anthroposophical Society for other members. It will become clear to you during the discussion of practical principles tomorrow that this can only be achieved through the adoption of certain definite measures. Naturally heirs should not suffer, but it is nevertheless possible, without prejudicing heirs, to make sure that one's property within the community cannot be inherited by

The Architecture of a Community in Dornach

any heir who is not a member of the Anthroposophical Society.

It would be most desirable to maintain this community into an indefinite future as one for members of the Anthroposophical Society. But it would not be at all in keeping with our spiritual movement only to have in mind how pleasant it is to be able to live there oneself, how nice it is not to have too far to go to performances and lectures in the Goetheanum, and how enjoyable it is to be among fellow anthroposophists. That our spiritual movement still requires a certain degree of sacrifice becomes doubly clear the moment the necessity arises to translate its principles and impulses into practical reality. It is more or less self-evident that we cannot have our houses built by architects at random; and it should be equally clear that we will try to preserve the anthroposophical character of the community.

These are aspects of the matter that I wanted to lay before you, not in order to exert pressure but as something which, on closer inspection, you will admit cannot be avoided if any significant results in the service of the Goetheanum building and thus of our anthroposophical concern are to be achieved at all.

An opportunity to create a model community

We had to abandon [*the proposed site in*] Munich, as you know, because we met in the first instance with absolutely no understanding for our artistic aims. In Dornach, where we are to be allowed to settle, we can put ourselves in a position to create a model for what our spiritual stream has to offer the future. We would be misunderstanding our movement if we did not want to do this, if we allowed petty considerations to prevent us from keeping to the views we have just discussed. Everyone who wants to build there ought to see the necessity of joining an association of the residents of our new Dornach community. Perhaps the best thing of all would be if the artistic side of the matter, in particular, were to be made subject to a kind of commission. There is no need to force this issue, but how splendid it would be if all the members of our new community were to agree to put everything destined to arise there in the hands of such a steering group.

Members of our community would then really be able to carry out our intention of filling a whole group with a common will and purpose, to be guided in the direction mapped out by our anthroposophical approach. In this way something really exemplary might arise in Dornach, and the result would show how well or how badly our cause had been understood. Every ugly house put up by one architect or another would be further proof of how little is understood as yet of our anthroposophical movement, while every house expressing our anthroposophical way of thinking in its forms would give rise to pleasure at this proof that at least some individuals do have an understanding of what we want to achieve!

Eurythmeum, 1923

A contribution to the world at large

It is my great wish to see the fulfilment of my intentions for this general meeting, and I still hope that we may make progress tomorrow on the questions of how each one of us might work amongst our fellow citizens in an anthroposophical way, and of how we could best show our attitude and place our experience at the service of society at large. Perhaps we can still have a really stimulating discussion about this. If we mean to gain ground in the world for our movement, it is not enough merely to show, on its own, the wisdom to be found in anthroposophy. In what we create in Dornach we must take pains to embody, for the world to see, what is given to us in the form of spiritual knowledge, just as older styles of architecture embodied bygone cultures.

Transformer station, 1921

If we are successful in creating something truly homogeneous in Dornach, and also in providing full legal security for it as the preserve of the anthroposophical movement, then we shall have offered proof of the fact that we have understood the aims of our movement. Let us hope that architectural and other artistic forms of many kinds will begin to prove to us that anthroposophy as such is being properly understood.

Most emphatically we do not want to be a sect or some group or other asserting its dogmas. We want to be something that takes cultural tasks seriously. So far as the Goetheanum and the buildings surrounding it are concerned, we can only do this if we act in accordance with what has been said.[2]

PART TWO

11. The Temple is the Human Being

The following lecture from 1911 is an early statement of Steiner's architectural intentions for the Goetheanum building, although the project had not yet acquired this title.[1] On this occasion he places the architectural task in the context of the history of temple building. At a certain point he refers to the legendary Solomon's Temple as having had the same aim as 'the temple of the future'. By this he means the building that became the Goetheanum; it being a first attempt to explore what this future temple might be like. Steiner is, therefore, connecting his work with one of the great mysteries of humanity, the legend of the 'lost temple' and its restoration. This temple is, as he says in the lecture, the human being. The Temple Legend itself is the subject of chapter 12.

In the building that is to be a home for spiritual science, full account must be taken of the evolutionary conditions and necessities of mankind as a whole. Unless this requirement is met, the aim of such a building will not be achieved. In an undertaking like this we have a deep responsibility to what we know to be the laws of the spiritual life, the powers of the spiritual world and the conditions of human evolution; and above all we must be mindful of the judgement that future times will make. In the present cycle of human evolution this responsibility is altogether different from what it was in times gone by.

Great creations of art and culture have many things to tell us of bygone ages. In a beautiful and impressive lecture this morning, you heard how they help us understand the inner constitution and attitude of the human soul in former times. Those who shared in the creation of ancient works of art had less burden of responsibility than we do today, because in ancient times human beings had at their disposal means of help which are no longer available in our epoch. In those days the gods let their forces stream into the subconscious life of human beings. So in a certain sense it is an illusion to believe that in the minds or souls of those who built the pyramids of Egypt, the temples of Greece and other great monuments only human thoughts were responsible for the impulses and aims expressed in the forms, the colours and so on. In those times the gods themselves were working through the hands, heads and hearts of human beings.

The fourth post-Atlantean epoch[2] now lies in the distant past, and our age is the first period of time in which the gods are putting the free creative activity of human beings to the test. They do not actually withhold their help, but they vouchsafe it only when human beings out of their own individual soul, developed through a number of incarnations, freely aspire to receive the forces streaming to them from above. What we have to create is essentially new, in the sense that we must work with forces that are altogether different from those obtaining in bygone times. We have to create out of the free activity of our own human souls. The hallmark of our age is consciousness, for it is the consciousness soul[3] which is the characteristic feature of the present epoch. If the future is to receive from us works of culture and of art such as we have received from the past, we must create out of full and clear consciousness, free from any influence arising out of our subconscious life. That is why we must open our minds and hearts to thoughts that shed light upon the task ahead of us. Only if we know upon what laws and fundamental spiritual impulses our work must be grounded, only if what we do is in line and harmony with the evolutionary forces operating in mankind as a whole, will achievement be within our reach.

A building that enshrines what is held most sacred

Let us now turn to certain basic ideas that can make our work fruitful in creating something that is fundamentally new, new in its very essence.

In a sense our intention is to build a temple that is also to be a place of teaching, as were the ancient temples of the mysteries. Buildings erected to enshrine what human beings have held most sacred have always been known as temples. You have already heard how the life of the human soul in the different epochs came to expression in temple buildings. When we study these buildings with insight and warmth of soul, differences are at once apparent. A very striking example is given by the forms of temples belonging to the second post-Atlantean epoch of culture. Outwardly, at any rate, very little is left of these ancient Persian temples, and their original form can only be dimly pictured or reconstructed from the Akashic Records.[4] Something reminiscent of their forms did indeed find its way into the later temples of the third epoch, into Babylonian-Assyrian architecture, and above all into the temples of Asia Minor, but only in those aspects that are typical of the region as such.

The most striking and significant feature of early architecture

Documentary records have little information to give on the subject. But if, assuming that investigation of the Akashic Records itself is not possible, we study the remains of buildings of a later epoch, gleaning from them some idea of what the earlier temples in that part of the world may have been like, we shall begin to realize that in these very ancient temples everything depended on the facade, on the impression made by the front of the temple on those who approached its portals. A person making his way through this facade into the interior of the temple would have felt that the facade spoke to him in a secret, mysterious language; in the interior of the temple he found everything that was striving to express itself in the

The Temple is the Human Being 217

Pyramids of Cheops (left) and Chefren (right), Gisa, Egypt

facade. He would have felt this no matter whether he came as a layman or as one who had been initiated.

Turning now from these temples—the character of which can only be dimly surmised by those unable to read the Akashic Records—to the temples of Egypt, or other sacred buildings such as the pyramids, we find something altogether different. Symbolic figures of mystery and grandeur stand before us as we approach an ancient

Corridor in pyramid of Cheops, 5 ft 9 in (1.75 m) high

Egyptian temple; the sphinx, the pyramids and even the obelisks are riddles—so much so that the German philosopher Hegel spoke of this art as the art of the 'enigma'.

The uprising form of the pyramid, in which there is scarcely an aperture, seems to enshrine a mystery; the outer facade presents us with a riddle. In the interior, we find

The Parthenon, Athens

indications of something that is to lead the hearts and souls of human beings to the god who dwelt in deep concealment within the innermost sanctuary. We also find information on manifold secrets written in the ancient mystery script, or what later took its place. While the temple enshrines the most sacred mystery—the mystery of the god—pyramids in their very architecture enshrine the mystery of the human being, of initiation, of which the inmost secrets must be hidden away from the external world.

The temples of Greece retain the basic principle of many Egyptian temples as dwelling places of the divine, spiritual presence. But the outer structure itself indicates a further stage. In the Greek temple's wonderful expression of dynamic power, not in the forms alone but in inner forces weaving in the forms, it is whole and complete, intrinsically perfect—an infinitude in itself. The Greek god dwells within this temple. In this building, the propor-

Sainte Chapelle, Paris

The Temple is the Human Being 221

tions of whose columns have an inner dynamic exactly suited to the weight they are intended to support, the god is enshrined in something that is whole and perfect in itself, that depicts in every detail, from the grandest to the tiniest, an infinitude in finite earthly existence.

The idea embodied in the Christian church is the temple as an expression of all that is most precious to human beings. Such buildings, erected originally over a grave, indeed over the grave of the Redeemer, later came to underpin a spire tapering upwards to the heights. In a church we have the expression of an altogether new impulse, whereby Christian temple architecture is distinguished from that of Greece. The Greek temple is self-sufficient, a single complete, dynamic whole. But a Christian church is quite different. I once said that by its very nature a temple dedicated to Pallas Athene, to Apollo or to Zeus needs no human being near it or inside it; it stands there in its own self-contained, solitary majesty as the dwelling-place of the god. The Greek temple is an infinitude in itself in that it is the dwelling-place of the god, so that the further away people are from it the truer it appears. Paradoxical as it may seem, this is the conception underlying the Greek temple. A Christian church is quite different. Its forms call out to the hearts and minds of the faithful. Every detail in the space we enter tells us that it exists in order to receive the congregation with all their thoughts, aspirations and feelings.

A Gothic church, with its characteristic forms, tries to

express something that is not as separate and complete in itself as a Greek temple. In each and every form Gothic architecture seems to reach out beyond its own boundaries, to express the aspirations and search of those within its walls; everywhere there is a kind of urge to break through the enclosing walls and mingle with the universe. The Gothic arch arose, of course, from a feeling for dynamic proportion. But apart from this there is something in all Gothic forms that seems to lead out and beyond; such forms strive to make themselves permeable. One of the reasons why a Gothic building makes its wonderful impression is that the many-coloured windows provide such a mysterious and yet such a natural link between the interior space and the all-pervading light. Could there be any sight in the world more radiant and glorious than that of the light streaming in through the stained glass windows of a Gothic cathedral among the dancing specks of dust? Could any enclosed space make a more majestic impression than this—where even the enclosing walls seem to lead out beyond themselves, where the interior space itself reaches out to the mysteries of infinite space?

The earliest temples of Asia Minor: a picture of the upright human form

This rapid survey of a lengthy period in the development of temple architecture has shown how this art

The Temple is the Human Being 223

develops in step with human evolution as though based on an underlying law. But for all that, we are still faced with a sphinxlike riddle. What is really at the root of it? Why has it developed in this specific way? Can any explanation be given for those remarkable fronts and facades covered with strange figures of winged animals or winged wheels, for the curious columns and capitals to be found in the region of Asia Minor as the last surviving fragments of the first stage of temple architecture? These fronts tell us something very remarkable; they tell us exactly the same, in a way, as is experienced within the temple itself. Can there be any greater enigma than the forms that are to be seen even today on fragments preserved in modern museums? What principle underlies it all?

There is an explanation, but it can only be found through insight into the thoughts and aims of those who participated in the building of these temples. This, of course, is a matter in which the help of spiritual vision is indispensable. What is a temple of Asia Minor in reality? Does its prototype or model exist anywhere in the world?

The following will indicate what this prototype is and throw light upon the whole subject. Imagine a human being lying on the ground, in the act of bringing his upper body and countenance upright. From a prostrate position the trunk is raised so that it may come into the vertical flow of downstreaming spiritual forces and be united with them. This image will give you an inkling of the inspiration from which the architectural forms of the early

Human-headed bull from Khorsabad, Assyria

The Temple is the Human Being 225

temples of Asia Minor were born. All the columns, capitals and remarkable figures of such temples are a symbolic expression of what we may feel at the sight of a human being raising himself upright, with all that is revealed by the movements of his hands, his features, the look on his face, and so on. If with the eyes of the spirit we were able to look behind this countenance into the inner human being, into the microcosm that is an image of the macrocosm, we should find—inasmuch as the countenance expresses the inner human being—that the countenance and the inner human being are related in the same way as the facade or front of a temple of Asia Minor was related to its interior.

A human being in the act of raising himself upright is what the early temple of Asia Minor expresses, not as a copy but as the underlying motif and all that this motif suggests. The spiritual picture given by anthroposophy of the physical nature of man helps us to realize the sense in which such a temple is an expression of the microcosm, of the human being. An understanding of the aspiring human being, therefore, sheds light on the fundamental character of that early architecture. The spiritual counterpart of the human being, as a physical being, is impressed on those remarkable temples of which only fragments and ruins have survived. This could be pointed out in every detail, down to the winged wheels and the original forms of all such designs. The temple is indeed the human being! This rings out to us across the ages like a clarion call.

Erechtheion, Athens: Caryatid Porch

The temples of Egypt and Greece: buildings permeated by soul

So what about the temples of Egypt and Greece? The human being can be described not only as a physical being but also as a being of soul. When we approach the human being on earth as a being of soul, all that we perceive at first in his eyes, his countenance, his gestures is a riddle as great in every respect as that presented by the Egyptian temple. Within the human being we find the holy of holies, accessible only to those who can find the way from the outer to the inner. There, in the innermost sanctuary, a human soul is concealed, just as the god and the secrets of the mysteries were concealed in the temples and pyramids of Egypt.

But the soul is not so deeply concealed in a human being as to be unable to find expression in his whole bearing and appearance. When the soul truly permeates the body, the body becomes the outward expression and manifestation of the soul. The human body is then revealed to us as a work of artistic perfection, permeated by soul, an infinitude complete in itself. Look for something in the visible world that is as whole and perfect in itself as the physical body of the human being permeated by his soul. In respect of dynamic perfection you will find nothing except the Greek temple which, in its self-contained perfection, is at the same time the dwelling-place and the expression of the god. In the sense that the human being, as microcosm, is a soul within a body, so the temple of Egypt and the temple of Greece is in reality the human being.

The human being raising himself upright is the prototype of the temple in Asia Minor. The human being standing on the earth, concealing a mysterious world within himself but able to let the forces of this inner world stream perpetually through his being, directing his gaze horizontally forward, closed in from above and below — that is the Greek temple. Again the annals of world history tell us that the temple is indeed the human being!

We are now approaching our own epoch. Its origin is to be found in the fruits of the ancient Hebrew culture and of Christianity, the Mystery of Golgotha, although initially the new impulse had to find its way through architectural forms handed down from Egypt and from Greece. But the urge was to break through these forms, to break through their boundaries in such a way that they led out beyond all enclosed space to the weaving life of the universe.

The mystery of Solomon's Temple

The seeds of whatever happens in the future have always been sown in the past. The temple of the future is foreshadowed, mysteriously, in the past. As I am speaking of something that is a perpetual riddle in the evolution of humanity, I can hardly do otherwise than speak of the riddle itself in rather enigmatic terms.

Reference is often made to Solomon's Temple. We know

The Temple is the Human Being 229

that it was meant to be an expression of the spiritual realities of human evolution. The enigma is that it is pointless to ask who has ever seen this Temple of Solomon about which such grand truths are uttered. Herodotus travelled in Egypt and the region of Asia Minor only a few centuries after the Temple of Solomon must have been built. From his account of his travels — which mentions matters of far less importance — we know that he must have passed within a few miles of Solomon's Temple, but did not set eyes on it. People had not yet seen this temple.

The enigma is that something certainly existed and yet had not been seen. But so it is. In nature, too, there is something that may be present and yet not seen. The comparison is not perfect, however, and to press it any further would lead wide of the mark. Plants are contained within their seeds, but human eyes do not see the plants within the seeds. This comparison, as I said, must not be pressed any further; for anyone attempting to base an explanation of Solomon's Temple upon it would immediately be saying something incorrect. In the way I have expressed it, however, the comparison between the seed of a plant and the Temple of Solomon is correct.

What is the aim of Solomon's Temple? Its aim is the same as that of the temple of the future.

Can we not, then, picture man spiritually as a human being lying on the ground and raising himself upright; then standing before us as a self-contained whole, a self-grounded, independent infinitude, with eyes gazing straight ahead; and finally as a human being whose gaze is directed to the heights, who raises his soul to the spirit which he is receiving. To say that the spirit is spiritual is tautology, but for all that, this underlines what is meant, namely, that the spirit is a supersensible reality.

Art, however, can work and be expressed only in the realm of the senses. In other words, the spirit that is received into the soul must be able to pour itself into form. Just as the human being raising himself upright, and then consolidated in himself, were prototypes of the ancient temples, so the prototype of the temple of the future must be the human soul into which the spirit is being received. The mission of our age is to found an architecture that will be able to say with clarity to people of the future that the temple is indeed the human being receiving the spirit into his soul.

The new temple: the incarnate spirit revealed

This new temple architecture will differ from all its predecessors, and this brings us back to what was said at the beginning of the lecture. With our physical eyes we can actually see a human being in the act of raising himself upright. But one whose being is suffused by soul must be inwardly felt, inwardly perceived. Merely looking is not enough. As you heard this morning, the sight of a Greek temple 'makes us aware in the very marrow of our bones'. Truly, the Greek temple lives within us because we *are* that temple, in so far as each of us is a microcosm permeated by soul. The quickening of the soul by the spirit is an invisible, supersensible fact, and yet it must become perceptible in the world of the senses if it is to be expressed in art.

No epoch except our own, and the one to come, could give birth to this form of art. Today we have to make a beginning, although it can be no more than that, an attempt—rather as when the temple which, having previously been whole and perfect in itself, strove in Christian churches to break through its own walls and make connection with the weaving life of the universe.

What do we need to build?

We need to build something that will bring to a culmination what has just been described. With the powers that spiritual science can awaken in each of us we must try to create an interior space which, in the effects produced by its colours, forms and other features, is a place set apart—but not shut off, for wherever we look our eyes and our hearts should be invited to penetrate through the walls. So that while secluded, as though within a sanctuary, we are at the same time at one with the weaving life of the divine. The temple that belongs truly to the future will have walls—and yet no walls. Its interior will have renounced every trace of egotism that may be associated with an enclosed space, and all its colours and forms will give expression to a selfless endeavour to receive the inpouring forces of the universe. At the inauguration of our building in Stuttgart I tried to indicate what can be achieved in this direction by colours and how colours can be the link with the spirits of the environment present in the spiritual atmosphere.[5]

Where is the supersensible aspect of the human being revealed to us within the physical body? Only when he speaks, when he pours his inner life of soul into the word; when the word is the embodiment of wisdom and prayer, entrusting itself to the human being as it enshrines cosmic mysteries. The word that becomes flesh within the human being is the spirit expressing itself in the physical body. We shall either create the building we ought to create, or we shall fail. If we fail, the task will have to be left to those who come after us. But we shall have succeeded if, for the first time, we give the interior space the most perfect form that is possible today, no matter what the outside appearance of the building may be. The exterior may or may not be prosaic; basically that is of no consequence. The outside appearance is there for the secular world, which is not concerned with the interior. It is the interior that is of importance, so what will it be like?

The interior: a union of form and content

At every turn our eyes will light upon something that says to us: This interior, with its language of colours and forms, in its whole living reality, is an expression of the word spoken in this place, that most spiritual element which the human being can enshrine within his physical body. The word that reveals the riddle of the human being in wisdom and in prayer will be at one, in this building, with the forms that surround the interior space. The words sent forth into this space will set their own range and boundaries, so that as they come up against the walls they will find something to which they are so attuned that what has issued from the human being will resound back into the space again. The dynamic power of the word will go forth from the centre to the periphery, and the interior space itself will then re-echo the proclamation and message of the spirit. This interior will be enclosed and yet open to infinitudes of spirit, though not by means of windows but by its very shape and form.[6]

12. The Restoration of the Lost Temple

The following is the first in a series of four lectures given in May 1905.[1] While this lecture may strike some as far removed from fields normally thought to relate to architecture, if we follow Steiner's more esoteric thoughts through to the end we can see how they connect with the deeper sources of his architectural work. Steiner speaks here of the ultimate development of all seven members of the human being. So far in this book we have met the fourfold human constitution. Ultimately, however, there will be a further three 'members' of our being evolving through transformation of the first three 'principles', as Steiner refers to them here (the physical, etheric and astral bodies) by the newest principle, the self-conscious ego, which, as the fourth principle at work in us, stands at the centre of the metamorphic sequence. When this transformation has been accomplished the human being will become completely spiritualized and the 'temple' of the human body and the earth will be restored.

As Steiner describes it here, building this temple requires the application of spiritual principles to every sphere of life. This is not a new idea of course and Steiner gives the example of the legendary seven kings of ancient Rome as representing the seven principles of the human being.

At the heart of the lecture and, it could be said, of Steiner's whole spiritual endeavour, is the legend of Cain and Abel (the Temple Legend), which to him represents two streams of humanity. The Sons of Cain '. . . are those who till the earth and create from inanimate nature and transform it through the arts of man'. Abel, on the other hand, '. . . held firmly to what he found, he took the world as it was'. The two streams are represented in the legend as Solomon and Hiram. Solomon, a descendent of Abel, embodied cosmic wisdom as given by the spiritual world – the world as created by God. Hiram, as Solomon's architect, had the task of transforming wisdom into earthly deed by building the temple.

Towards the end of the lecture, Steiner says that 'When man learns to create with the same wisdom with which the divine powers have created nature and made physical things, then will the temple be built [on earth].*' As we have seen in earlier chapters of this book, this is the same thought which, some eight years later, led to the laying of the foundation stone for the first Goetheanum, in 1913. It is also the leading thought behind the social initiative that Steiner took at Christmas 1923, when he refounded the General Anthroposophical Society.[2] Apart from being an internal exercise in restructuring the anthroposophical movement, Steiner was aware of the urgent need to create social forms that could nurture a new culture based on spiritual freedom. This need is, of course, even more urgent today.*

Today we will explain a great allegory, and deal with an object that is known to occult science as the image or teaching of the lost temple which has to be rebuilt. I have explained in earlier lectures why in occult science one starts from such images. Today we shall see what an enormous number of ideas are contained in essence in this image. In doing so I will also have to touch on a theme that is much misunderstood by those who know little or nothing about theosophy. There are some people who do not understand that theosophy and practical, everyday things go hand in hand, that they must work together throughout the whole of life. Therefore I shall have to speak about the connection between theosophy[3] and the practical things of life. For, basically, when we take up the theme of the lost temple which has to be rebuilt we are speaking about everyday work.

This means that I shall, indeed, be in the position of a teacher who prepares his pupils for building a tunnel. The building of a tunnel is something eminently practical. Someone might well say: 'Building a tunnel is simple; one only has to start digging into a hill from one side and to excavate away until one emerges at the other side.' Everyone can see that it would be foolish to think in this way. But in other realms of life that is not always perceived. Whoever wishes to build a tunnel must, of course, first of all have a command of higher mathematics. Then he will have to learn how the tunnel is to be built, technically. Without practical engineering knowledge, without the art of ascertaining the right level, one would not be able to keep on course in excavating a tunnel through a mountain. Then one also needs to know basic geological concepts, understand the various rock strata, the direction of water courses and metal lodes in the mountain, and so on. It would be foolish to think that someone would be

The Restoration of the Lost Temple 237

able to build a tunnel without all this prior knowledge, or that an ordinary stone mason could construct a whole tunnel.

It would be just as foolish to believe that one could begin building human society by drawing solely on perspectives offered by ordinary life. Yet this folly is perpetrated by many people, and in countless books. Everyone today supposes himself to know and be entitled to decide how best to reform social life and the state. People who have hardly learnt anything write detailed books about how society should best be organized, and feel themselves called upon to found reform movements. Thus there are movements for reform in all spheres of life. But everything done in this way is just the same as if someone were to try to cut a tunnel with hammer and chisel. It is all a result of not knowing that great laws exist that hold sway in the world and arise from the life of the spirit.

The real problem of our times consists in this ignorance [*of the fact*] that there are profound laws governing the building of a state and of the social organism, just as there are for building a tunnel, and that one must know these laws in order to carry out the most necessary and everyday tasks in the social organism. Just as in building a tunnel one has to know about the interaction of all the forces of nature, so anyone wishing to start reforming society must know the laws underlying interactions between people, human relationships. One must study the effect of one soul on another, and draw near to the spirit. That is why theosophy must underpin every practical activity in life. Theosophy is the real practical principle of life; and only those who start from theosophical principles and carry them into practical life can really develop a capacity to affect social conditions.

That is why theosophy should penetrate all spheres of life. Statesmen, social reformers and the like are nothing without a theosophical basis, without theosophical principles. That is why, for those who study these things, all work in this field, everything done today to develop the fabric of society, is external tinkering and complete chaos. For one who understands the matter, what social reformers are doing today is like somebody cutting stones and piling them one on top of another in the belief that a house will thereby arise of its own accord. First of all a plan of the house must be drawn up. It is just the same if one asserts that, in social life, things will take shape of their own accord. One cannot reform society without knowing the laws of theosophy.

This way of thinking, which works according to an underlying plan and sense of spiritual laws, can be traced back to medieval Freemasons, who dealt with and made contracts with the clergy about how they should build, and wanted nothing else than to shape outer life in such a way that—along with the Gothic cathedral—it could become an image of the great spiritual structure of the universe. Take the Gothic cathedral. Though composed of thousands of individual parts, it is built according to a single idea, much more comprehensive than the cathedral itself. To become complete in itself, divine life must flow

The Restoration of the Lost Temple 239

into it, just as light shines into the church through the multicoloured windows. And when the medieval priest spoke from the pulpit, so that divine light shone in his listener's hearts just like the light shining through the coloured windows, then the resonances of the preacher's words were in harmony with the great life of God. The life of such a sermon, born out of the life of the spirit, spread further than the cathedral itself. In like manner, nowadays, the whole of external life should be transformed into the temple of the earth, into an image of the whole spiritual structure of the universe.

If we go still further back in time, we find that it is this same way of thinking which held sway in mankind from the very earliest times. Let me explain what I mean by way of an example. In our epoch there is much chaotic interaction between one human being and another. Each individual pursues his own aims. But in former times things were different. I have often spoken about the cultural epochs within our fifth great epoch.[4] The first of these was the ancient Indian epoch, the second, that of the Medes and the Persians, the third, that of the Babylonians, the Assyrians, the Chaldeans, the Egyptians and the Semites; and the fourth was the Graeco-Roman period. We are now in the fifth epoch.[5]

The fourth and fifth cultural epochs were the first ones to be based on the intelligence of human beings, of individuals. In art we find a great monument to the conquest of ancient priestly culture by individual human intelligence—the *Laocoon*.[6] The *Laocoon* priest entwined with serpents—the symbol of subtlety—symbolizes the conquest by a culture of individual human intelligence of the old priestly civilization, which held other views about truth and wisdom and about what should happen. Here we have the overcoming of the third cultural epoch by the fourth, also represented in another symbol, in the saga of the Trojan Horse. The cunning intelligence of Odysseus created the Trojan horse, by means of which Trojan priestly culture was overthrown. [...]History likewise speaks of seven Roman kings: Romulus, Numa Pompilius, Tullus Hostihus, Ancus Martius, Tarquinius Priscus, Servius Tullius and Tarquinius Superbus. Following Livy's account it used to be believed that the first seven kings of Rome were real personalities. Today, historians know that these first seven kings never existed. We are therefore dealing with a legend or saga, but historians have no inkling of what lies behind it, for the veil spread over the priestly culture of earliest Roman history can only be lifted by theosophy.

The seven Roman kings represent nothing else than the seven constituent principles of the human being as we know them from theosophy. Just as the human organism consists of seven parts—physical body, etheric body, astral body, 'I' or ego, then higher Manas [*Spirit Self*], Buddhi [*Life Spirit*] and Atma [*Spirit Man*], so the social organism was conceived, as it took shape at the time, as a sequence in seven stages. And only if it developed according to the law of the number seven, which underlies all nature, was it able to prosper. Thus the rainbow has seven colours: red, orange, yellow, green, blue, indigo, violet. Likewise there are seven intervals in the scale: first, second, third, fourth, fifth, and so on. Likewise the atomic weights in chemistry follow the rule of the number seven. And this permeates the whole of creation.

Hence it was self-evident to guardians of ancient wisdom that the structure of human society must also be regulated by such a law. According to a precisely developed plan, these seven kings are seven stages, seven integral parts of the whole. This was the usual way of inaugurating a new epoch in history at that time. A plan was devised, since this was considered a means of preventing foolish aberrations, and a law was written to embody it. This plan was actually there at the outset. In ancient times everyone knew that world history was guided according to a fixed plan. Everyone knew that, for instance, in the third phase of the fourth epoch, they would have to be guided by this and that principle. And so, at first, in ancient Rome one still had a priestly state with a plan underlying its culture, written down in books called the Sibylline Books. These are nothing other than the original plan underlying the law of the sevenfold epoch, and they were still consulted when needed in the earliest days of the Roman Empire.

The physical body was taken as a model for these foundations. That is not so unreasonable. Today people are inclined to treat the physical body as something subordinate. People look down on the physical with a kind of disdain. Yet this is not justified, because our physical body is actually our most exalted part. Take a single bone. Take a good look at the upper part of a thighbone and you will see how wonderfully it is constructed. The best engineer, the greatest technician, could not produce anything so perfect if he were set the task of attaining the greatest possible strength using the least amount of material. And so the whole human body is constructed in the most perfect way. This physical body is really the most perfect thing imaginable. An anatomist will always speak with the utmost admiration of the human heart, which functions in a wonderful way, even though human beings do little else throughout life than imbibe what is poison for it. Alcohol, tea, coffee and so on attack the heart in the most destructive fashion. But so wonderfully has this organ been built that it can withstand all this into ripe old age.

The physical body, the lowest of the bodies, therefore possesses the greatest perfection. Less perfect, on the other hand, are the higher bodies, which have not yet gained such perfection in their development. The etheric body and the astral body continually offend against our physical body through the attacks of our lust, desires and wishes.[7] Then follows, as the fourth principle, the real baby of them all, the human 'I' or ego, which like a wandering will-o'-the-wisp must await a future time for those laws that will act as a guide for its conduct, just as the physical body was informed by its laws a long time ago.

When we develop a social structure, we must have a principle that renders its foundations firm. Thus the saga of the seven kings allows Romulus, the first Roman king,

The Restoration of the Lost Temple 243

who represents the first principle [*physical reality*], to be raised to heaven as the god Quinnus. The second king, Numa Pompilius, the second [*etheric or life*] principle, embodies social order; he brought laws for the conduct of ordinary life, and for everything of a habitual nature, connected with social custom. The third king, Tullus Hostilius, represents the passions. Under him, the attacks against divine nature begin, causing discord, struggle and war, through which Rome became great. Under the fourth king, Ancus Martius, the arts develop, which spring from the human ego.

Now the four lower principles of man are not able to give birth to the three higher principles, the fifth, sixth and seventh. This is also symbolized in Roman history. The fifth Roman king, Tarquinius Priscus, was not engendered out of the Roman 'organism' as such, but was introduced into Roman culture from Etruscan culture as something higher. The sixth king, Servius Tullus, represents the sixth member of the human cyclic law, Buddhi. He is able to rule over kama [*the astral body*], the physical-sensual counterpart of Buddhi. He represents the canon of the law. The seventh king, Tarquinius Superbus, the most exalted principle, is he who must be overthrown, since it is not possible to maintain the high level, the impulse, of the social system.[8]

We see demonstrated in Roman history, therefore, the fact that there must be a plan underlying the architecture and edifice of the state, just as for any other building in the world. That the world is a temple, that social life must be structured and organized, and must have pillars like a temple, and that the great sages must be these pillars—it is this intention which is permeated by ancient wisdom. This is not a wisdom that is merely learned, but one that has to be *built into* human society.

Only those who fully absorb all this knowledge, all this wisdom, can really build a sound social structure. We would not achieve much as theosophists if we were to restrict ourselves to contemplating how the human being is built up from his different active principles. No, we are only able to fulfil our task if we carry the principles of theosophy into everyday life. We must learn to put them to use in such a way that every turn of the hand, every movement of a finger, every step we take, bears the impress, is an expression of the spirit. In that case we shall be engaged in building the lost temple.

Along with that, however, goes the fact, which I mentioned recently, that we should take into ourselves something of the greatness and all-embracing comprehensiveness of universal laws. Our habits of thought must be permeated by that kind of wisdom which leads from great conceptions into details—in the same way as house construction starts from the finished and complete plan, rather than from laying one stone upon another. This is necessary if our world is not to subside into chaos. As theosophists we should recognize the fact that law is bound to rule in the world as soon as we realize that every step we make, every action of ours, is like an impression stamped in wax by the spiritual world. Then we shall be

The Restoration of the Lost Temple 245

engaged in the building of the temple. That is the meaning of temple building: whatever we set ourselves to do must be in conformity to inner law.

It has increasingly been forgotten that man needs to include himself in the construction of the great world temple. A person can be born and die today without having any inkling of the fact that laws are working in us, and that everything we do is governed by the laws of the universe. The whole of modern life is wasted when people do not know that they have to live according to laws. Therefore the priestly sages of ancient times devised means of rescuing, for the new culture, something of the great laws of the spiritual world. It was, so to speak, a stratagem of the great sages to have hidden this order and harmony in many branches of life—yes, right down to the games people played as recreation at the end of the day. In playing cards, in the figures of chess, in the sense of the rules by which one plays, we find a hint, if only a faint one, of the order and harmony that I have described. When you sit down with someone to a game of cards, it will not do if you do not know the rules, the manner of playing. And this really conveys a hint of the great laws of the universe. What is known as the sephirot of the Cabbala, what we know as the seven principles in their various forms, can be rediscovered in the way in which cards are laid down, one after the other, in the course of a game. At least those who can play cards will not wholly waste their present incarnation!

These are secrets ways in which the great initiates

intervene in the wheel of existence. If one told people to follow great cosmic laws, they would not comply. But if the laws are introduced unnoticed into things, it is often possible to inject a drop of this attitude into them. If you have this attitude, then you will have a notion of what is symbolized in the mighty allegory of the lost temple. In secret societies, including that of Freemasonry, something connected with the lost temple and its future reconstruction has been described in the 'Temple Legend'. The Temple Legend is very profound, but even modern Freemasons usually have no notion of it. A Freemason is not much different from the majority of people ... but if he lets the Temple Legend work upon him, this is a great help for the future. For whoever absorbs the Temple Legend receives something which, in a specific way, shapes his thinking in an orderly fashion. And everything depends on ordered thinking. This Temple Legend I have spoken of goes as follows.

Once one of the Elohim[9] united with Eve, and out of that Cain was born. Another of the Elohim, Adonai or Jehovah-Yahveh, thereupon created Adam. The latter, for his part, united with Eve, and out of this marriage Abel was born. Adonai caused trouble between those belonging to Cain's family and those belonging to Abel's family, and the result of this was that Cain slew Abel. But out of the renewed union of Adam with Eve the race of Seth was founded.

Thus we have two different races of mankind. The one consists of the original descendants of the Elohim, the sons of Cain, who are called the Sons of Fire. They are those

The Restoration of the Lost Temple 247

who till the earth and create from inanimate nature, transforming it through the arts of man. Enoch, one of the descendants of Cain, taught mankind the art of hewing stone, of building houses, of organizing society, of founding civilized communities. Another of Cain's descendants was Tubal-Cain, who worked in metal. The architect Hiram-Abiff was descended from the same race.

Abel was a shepherd. He held firmly to what he found, taking the world as it was 'given'. One frequently finds this antithesis between people. One sticks to things as they are, the other wants to create new life from the inanimate, through art. Other nations have portrayed the ancestor of these Sons of Fire in the Prometheus saga. It is the Sons of Fire who have to bring divine wisdom, beauty and goodness down from all-embracing universal thought, in order to transform the world into a temple.

King Solomon was a descendant of the lineage of Abel. He could not build the temple himself, for he lacked the art to do so. Hence he appointed the architect Hiram-Abiff, the descendant of the lineage of Cain. Solomon was divinely handsome. When the Queen of Sheba met him, she thought she saw an image of gold and ivory. She came to unite herself with him.

Jehovah is also called the God who turns the life principle into form, in contrast with that other Elohim who creates by charming life out of what is lifeless. To which of these does the future belong? That is the great question of the Temple Legend. If mankind were to develop under the religion of Jehovah, all life would become fixed in form and expire. In occult science, this is called the 'Transition to the Eighth Sphere'. But the point in time has now arrived when man himself must awaken what is dead to life. That will happen through the Sons of Cain, through those who do not rely on the things around them but are themselves the creators of new forms. The Sons of Cain themselves construct the world's edifice.

When the Queen of Sheba saw the temple and asked who the architect was, she was told it was Hiram. And as soon as she saw him, he seemed to her to be the one who was predestined for her. King Solomon now became jealous; and indeed, he entered into league with three apprentices who had failed to achieve their master's degree, and sought to undermine Hiram's great masterpiece, the Molten Sea. This great masterpiece of casting was to arise through human spirit uniting with metal. Of the three apprentices, one was a Syrian mason, the second was a Phoenician carpenter, and the third was a Hebrew miner. The plot succeeded; the casting was destroyed by pouring water over it. It all blew apart. In despair the architect was about to throw himself into the heat of the flames. Then he heard a voice from the centre of the earth. This came from Cain himself, who called out to him: 'Take here the hammer of the world's divine wisdom, with which you must put all right again.' And Cain gave him the hammer. Now this is the human spirit which man builds into his astral body if he is not to let it remain in the condition in which he received it. This is the work that Hiram now

The Restoration of the Lost Temple 249

had to do. But there was a plot against his life. We shall proceed from here next time.

I wanted to recount the legend up to this point, to show how in the original occult brotherhoods there lived the idea that man has a task to fulfil — the task of recreating the inanimate world, of not being satisfied with what is already there. Wisdom thus becomes deed through penetrating the inanimate world, so that it becomes a reflection of original and eternal spirituality.

Wisdom, beauty and strength are the three fundamental words underlying all Freemasonry that is truly aware of its spiritual aims. Its task is to change the external world in such a way that it becomes a garment for the spiritual. Today, Freemasons themselves no longer understand this, and believe that man should work on his own ego. They regard themselves as particularly clever when they say that the working masons of the Middle Ages were not Freemasons. But the working masons were precisely those who have always been Freemasons, because their aim was to make outward structure a replica of the spiritual, of the temple of the world, which is to be constructed out of intuitive wisdom. This is the idea that formerly underpinned the great works of architecture, and was carried through into every detail.

I will give an example to illustrate the superiority of wisdom over mere intellect. Think of an old Gothic cathedral, and consider its wonderful acoustics, which cannot be matched today because this profound knowledge has been lost.

The famous Lake Moeris in Egypt is a similarly miraculous achievement of the human spirit. It was not a natural lake but was constructed through the intuition of the wise, so that water could be stored in times of flood for distribution over the whole country in time of drought. That was a great feat of irrigation.

When man learns to create with the same wisdom with which the divine powers have created nature and made physical things, then the temple will be built [*on earth*] ... we must develop the attitude of mind that knows that it is only through wisdom that the temple of all humanity can be created.

When today we go about in the cities, we find a shoe shop here, there a chemist, further on a cheesemonger and then a shop selling walking-sticks. If we do not want to buy anything at present, these separate shops do not concern us. How little the external life of a city reflects what we feel, think and perceive! Yet how very different it was in the Middle Ages. If a person walked through the streets in those days he saw the house fronts built in the resident's style, manner and character. Every doorknob expressed what the inhabitant had lovingly shaped in accordance with his spirit. Go, for instance, through a town such as Nuremberg; there you will still find the remains of how it used to be. And then, by contrast, examine the fashionable abstraction that no longer has anything to do with people, in this age of materialism and its chaotic products to which we have gradually come from an earlier spiritual epoch.

The Restoration of the Lost Temple 251

Man was born from a natural world that was once formed by the gods so that everything within it fitted the great scheme of the world, the great temple. There was once a time when there was nothing on this earth upon which you could gaze without having to say to yourself: Divine beings have built this temple to the stage in which the human physical body was perfected.

Then the higher principles of man's nature took possession of it, and disarray and chaos came into the world. Wishes, desires and emotions brought disarray into the temple of the world. Only when, out of man's own will, law and order once again speak in a loftier and more beautiful way than the gods once did in creating nature, only when man allows the god within him to arise, so that like a god he can work to build the temple—only then will the lost temple be regained.

It would not be right if we were to think that only those able to build should do so. No, it depends upon our attitude of mind, even if we know a great deal. If one has the right direction to one's thinking and then engages in social, technical and legal reforms, then one is building the lost temple which is to be rebuilt. But should one start reforms—however well-intended they may be—lacking this attitude of mind, then one is only bringing about more chaos, for an individual stone is useless if it does not fit into the overall plan [*of the building*]. Reform of the law, religion or anything else—as long as you only take account of the particular field without having an understanding of the whole—only results in demolition.

Theosophy is not just theory, but practice, the most practical thing in the world. It is a fallacy to suppose that theosophists are recluses, not engaged in shaping the world. If we could get people to engage in social reform on a theosophical basis, they would achieve much of what they want swiftly and surely. Particular movements only lead to fanaticism if pursued in isolation. All separate reform movements—emancipators, vegetarians, animal rights campaigners and so forth—are only useful if they all work together. Their ideal can only be properly realized in a great universal movement that leads through unity to the universal world temple.

That is the idea underlying the allegory of the lost temple which has to be rebuilt.

Notes

Introduction
1. For a comprehensive treatment of expressionist architecture and Steiner's relationship to it, see Wolfgang Pehnt, *Expressionist Architecture*; Dennis Sharp, *Modern Architecture and Expressionism*; and Biesantz/Klingborg, *The Goetheanum – Rudolf Steiner's Architectural Impulse*.
2. In relation to the task he saw for the anthroposophical movement, Steiner said: 'We have to realize that so long as we are compelled to hold our meetings in halls whose forms belong to a dying culture, our work will more or less inevitably share in the fate of all that is caught up in this decline.' (Stuttgart, 3 January 1911.)
3. In: *The Modulor – A Harmonious Measure to the Human Scale Universally Applicable to Architecture and Mechanics*.
4. See, for example, Tuchman et al., *The Spiritual in Art: Abstract Painting 1890–1985*.
5. Quoted in Peter Blundell-Jones, *Hans Scharoun*.
6. See, for example, *An Outline of Esoteric Science*.
7. Steiner referred to these stages as Old Saturn, Old Sun, Old Moon, the present Earth, Jupiter, Venus and Vulcan. Each of them refers to a spiritual condition and not to the planets as they appear physically in our present solar system.
8. Lecture of 29 December 1914 — see chapter 1.
9. The physical body is one among many examples of forms created by the dynamic processes of the etheric world. The most 'physical' aspect of the body, the skeleton, can be seen

as the outcome of movement which has come to rest. Rhythmic, dynamic movement is characteristic of any liquid-based process, of which the blood circulation is the prime example in the human body. In nature, the effects of the activity of the etheric world are visible in all water processes: tides, waves, vortexes, river estuaries etc. A comprehensive study of these 'forming processes' can be found in Theodor Schwenk, *Sensitive Chaos — The Creation of Flowing Forms in Water and Air*. See also note 1 to chapter 6.
10 See note 7 and also chapter 12.
11 The underlying spiritual form of the physical body is one of the themes of a lecture series given in 1911, published as *From Jesus to Christ*. In these lectures Steiner describes the resurrection body of Christ as the prototype of the future spiritualized physical body.

Chapter 1

1 Steiner is here referring to the activity of the spiritual beings known in Christian esotericism as Seraphim, Cherubim and Thrones, whom he describes as giving birth to time and space during the Old Saturn period of evolution.
2 From lecture given on 30 December 1914, published in *Art as Seen in the Light of Mystery Wisdom*.
3 See the introduction for an outline of the four 'members' of the human being as characterized by Steiner: the 'I' or 'ego', as self-conscious individuality, which is described here as holding a thought; the 'astral body', which carries our waking consciousness and, along with this, our impulses and desires; our 'etheric' or life body, which animates the fourth, fundamentally unconscious member — the physical body.

4   From lecture given on 29 December 1914, published in *Art as Seen in the Light of Mystery Wisdom*.
5   Steiner is referring to two spiritual beings whose names are derived from ancient traditions. 'Lucifer', a powerful expansive being of light, desires to draw us out of our bodies to enjoy a blissful existence free from the forces of gravity which weigh down both body and soul. 'Ahriman' on the other hand (a being known, originally, to the Zarathustran Mysteries of ancient Persia) is the polar opposite of Lucifer and tries to confine us to the forces of gravity, with their tendency to obliterate the light of the spirit in the darkness of matter, in both a physical and soul-spiritual sense.

   We live in a dynamic relationship between these polar forces: between 'levity' and weight; light and darkness. The 'superior ruler, who eternally brings about the balance between them' is Christ, who, in Steiner's cosmology, is the archetype of the human being.
6   From lecture given on 2 January 1915, published in *Art as Seen in the Light of Mystery Wisdom*.

Chapter 2

1   In using the term 'occultism' Steiner is referring to the investigation of phenomena which are 'occult' in the sense of being inaccessible, or hidden, to normal sense perception. In this context he is referring to the use of such knowledge to create forms in the physical world which the spiritual aspect of the human being will unconsciously respond to. In his view the forms of the gothic cathedrals were created by architects who had access to such knowledge. Nowadays the term 'occult' evokes mystical prac-

tices, and Steiner was at pains to point out that a modern path of spiritual investigation should begin with the faculties of common sense and a search for truth on which modern science is based. He was, however, striving to extend the boundaries of modern science. As he put it: 'It is the intention of spiritual science to free the methods and attitudes of scientific research from their particular application to the relationships and processes of sensory facts while preserving their way of thinking and other attributes.' (*An Outline of Esoteric Science*.)

2 Steiner appears to be saying that the forms of Gothic cathedrals affected the facial expressions (countenances) of people who absorbed them, presumably during their lifetimes. This point is rather confused with his wider statement that the 'entire human shape' is formed by the soul impressions made by architectural forms over thousands of years, i.e., over more than one lifetime. This latter point is similar to Steiner's discussion of illness conditions arising in the soul life in one incarnation and appearing as physical conditions in the following incarnation. In both cases, a soul experience has descended into the physical body. See Steiner: *Manifestations of Karma*.

3 Steiner describes the Atlantean epoch as the fourth in a group of seven stages which together are one of several subdivisions of the present 'Earth condition' of evolution. We are currently living in the fifth period in this group, which Steiner referred to as the 'post-Atlantean great epoch'. See, for example, chapter 4 of *An Outline of Esoteric Science*.

4 From lecture given on 14 September 1907, published in *Occult Signs and Symbols*.

Chapter 3

1. Steiner identified seven 'cultural epochs' during the present 'post-Atlantean great epoch' (see footnote 3 to chapter 2): the Ancient Indian, the Ancient Persian, the Egyptian Chaldean, the Graeco-Roman, the present fifth post-Atlantean cultural epoch, the sixth cultural epoch, and the seventh cultural epoch. For a fuller account see, for example, chapter 4 of *An Outline of Esoteric Science*.
2. From lecture given on 4 August 1908, published in *Universe Earth and Man*.
3. Steiner is pointing to the particularly strong way in which the Gothic period involved the contribution of craftsmen who were given a creative freedom that was new to temple building.
4. From lecture given on 17 June 1914, in *Architecture as a Synthesis of the Arts*.
5. From lecture of 4 August 1908, published in *Universe Earth and Man*.

Chapter 4

1. See chapter 1, note 5.
2. See chapter 1, note 5.
3. From lecture given on 28 June 1914, published in 'Ways to a new style in architecture' in *Architecture as a Synthesis of the Arts*.

Chapter 5

1. Art as research can take many forms. The saying of Goethe quoted here could be applied, for example, to the painter G. M. W. Turner whose work can be seen as a lifetime's research into the relationship between light, form and

atmosphere. Turner was, in fact, a contemporary of Goethe and studied his Theory of Colour. More recently, the modern movement in painting can be seen as research into many fundamental questions of form and colour, especially in its pioneering phase. A good contemporary example of the use of art as an extension of scientific research based on Goethe's scientific method is Colquoun and Ewald's *New Eyes for Plants*.

2 Steiner here refers to the 'Akashic Records', which exist only in spiritual reality. All thoughts and deeds throughout the ages are inscribed into the fabric of this cosmic memory and retained there. The spiritual researcher or initiate can investigate past ages of humanity by 'reading' in the vast book of these records.

3 In referring to human evolution here, Steiner is also using the sun and earth motifs as images of man's descent from spirit into matter (sun motif) and his subsequent state of being bound to the earth, as he expressed it earlier in the lecture (earth motif).

4 Steiner is probably referring to the artistic work being undertaken at the time in connection with the building of the first Goetheanum.

5 From lecture given on 7 June 1914, in *Architecture as a Synthesis of the Arts*.

Chapter 6

1 For a contemporary approach to research into metamorphosis, see, for example, Colquoun and Ewald's *New Eyes for Plants*.

2 Steiner was involved with the Theosophical Society from 1902 when he was asked to address a group of theosophists in

Berlin. For some years the Theosophical Society provided a forum in which he could develop his work, but tensions developed, particularly regarding the practical application of esoteric knowledge, as can be inferred from this excerpt. Finally, a fundamental difference with the leadership around Annie Besant, the President, led to Steiner's expulsion from the society in 1912. He then founded the Anthroposophical Society, together with most of the people who had formed the German membership of the Theosophical Society.

3 Berlin, 12 June 1907.
4 A more recent study of metamorphosis in the skeleton is L. F. C. Mees, *Secrets of the Skeleton – Form in Metamorphosis*.
5 Steiner means that the spiritual perceptions in this realm are more akin to hearing than seeing.
6 The designations used here are those which give their names to the days of the week. Although Steiner is clearly seeing the columns as representing the seven 'planetary conditions' of evolution, the names differ from those he commonly used in this connection (see note 7 in the Introduction to this book). In terms of the 'weekday' names, as Steiner uses them here, the central planet 'Mars' stands for the present 'earth' stage of evolution. Our own stage of evolution is therefore followed by 'Mercury', the planet which, in ancient wisdom, stands for movement and change including, one might say, metamorphosis. See also the illustration in chapter 8, showing how the Mercury motif appeared later in the first Goetheanum building.
7 Presumably a form with very little 'astral' quality, such as we find in the purely etheric life of plants.
8 From a folder of illustrations dated October 1907. Translation by Rex Raab.

9 See chapter 1, note 5.
10 See illustration on page 131 for example.
11 Whereas the ahrimanic had to be removed from the temple or House of the Word, it has its essential place in buildings with a more functional place, such as the boiler-house.
12 From lecture given on 4 January 1915, published in *Art as Seen in the Light of Mystery Wisdom*.

Chapter 7

1 Steiner's view of architecture as a synthesis of the arts is close to the expressionists' idea of the *Gesamtkunstwerk* (total work of art) of which Richard Wagner, for example, was an exponent. For both Wagner and Steiner, the synthesis embraced the visual and the performing arts together. Apart from Steiner's Goetheanum buildings, a built example was Hans Poelzig's Grosses Schauspielhaus (Great Theatre), built in Berlin in 1919 (unfortunately demolished in 1980).
2 This building had an oval space in the basement which had two sets of seven columns with capitals based on those used in the 1907 Congress (see chapter 6).
3 From lecture given on 2 January 1915, published in *Art as Seen in the Light of Mystery Wisdom*.
4 From lecture given on 7 June 1914, published in *Architecture as a Synthesis of the Arts*.
5 In Steiner's understanding of evolution the biblical 'Paradise' is a picture of a time when the human body still had a spiritual form and the earth was a cloudlike body. In other words, Paradise is a state that still hovers *above* earthly reality as we know it. For a fuller explanation of Steiner's understanding of the 'Fall' see, for example, chapter 4 of *An Outline of Esoteric Science*.

6   From lecture given on 17 June 1914 in *Architecture as a Synthesis of the Arts*.
7   Steiner uses the single word *Stimmung*.
8   'Elemental beings' are beings active in the four elements, out of which, according to ancient wisdom, everything in the physical world is formed: Fire/warmth (Salamanders), Air/gas (Sylphs), Water/liquid (Undines), and Earth/mineral (Gnomes). Later in this talk Steiner refers to other groups of beings related to the four 'kingdoms' of nature: minerals, plants, animals and human beings (in the sense that the human being is part of nature).
9   Here Steiner is talking about a different blue to the ultramarine used in the room in Stuttgart. As all painters know, different shades of a colour are experienced differently and the same colour is also experienced differently in different contexts. From his earlier remarks it follows that these variations of colour and context would involve different elemental beings.
10 The future transformation of the human being discussed in chapter 12 begins with the transformation of the human astral body. This is initiated by the spiritual element in the human being, the conscious ego, taking hold of the 'life of passion', as it is expressed here.
11 Talk given at the dedication of the new building for anthroposophy in Stuttgart, 15 October 1911.

Chapter 8

1 See chapter 1, note 5.
2 The wooden sculpture was made by Steiner in collaboration with the English sculptress Edith Maryon. Standing nine metres (30 feet) high, it is now housed in the second

Goetheanum building in Dornach. The work itself is complex and is the subject of *Rudolf Steiner's Sculpture.*
3   There was also a lectern placed at the intersection of the two domes.
4   Steiner himself wrote four such Mystery Plays, which gave artistic expression to ideas about karma, destiny, reincarnation and human relationships.
5   A new art of movement developed by Steiner, which aims to reveal the innate gestures of speech and music in visible form.

Chapter 9
1   The first Goetheanum originated as a project for a building which would have been buried in the middle of a city block in Munich but failed to get planning permission. Transferring the design to the site at Dornach in Switzerland was a late development. See also the introduction to chapter 11, note 1.
2   Steiner refounded the General Anthroposophical Society at Christmas 1923, a year after the burning of the first building. At this 'Christmas Foundation Meeting' he presented his model of the second building. A number of books have been written about the significance of this event. See, for example, Rudolf Grosse, *The Christmas Foundation – Beginning of a New Cosmic Age.*

Chapter 10
1   See chapter 8, note 5.
2   Lecture given in Berlin on 23 January 1914, published in *Architecture as a Synthesis of the Arts.*

Chapter 11

1 The lecture was given at the inaugural meeting of the Building Association, the organization that became responsible for financing and managing the Goetheanum building project. The original intention was to build a centre for anthroposophical work in Munich. See also note 1 to chapter 9.
2 See chapter 3, note 1.
3 A technical term in Steiner's anthroposophy, in the evolution of soul through 'sentient soul', 'mind soul' to 'consciousness soul'. In our present, consciousness-soul age, we can develop the capacity to act out of our own conscious self-reflection and individual decision.
4 See chapter 5, note 2.
5 This is a reference to the talk reproduced in chapter 7.
6 Lecture given on 12 December 1911, published in *Architecture as a Synthesis of the Arts*.

Chapter 12

1 The four lectures referred to here are part of a collection of 20 lectures given in Berlin between 1904 and 1906, published under the title of *The Temple Legend and the Golden Legend*. The lectures are connected with an Esoteric School which Steiner led from 1904 until 1914.
2 See note 2 to chapter 9. As we saw in chapter 9, the outward-facing gesture of the second Goetheanum building is intimately related to the social aims of the Christmas Foundation Meeting of 1923. An essential ingredient in this relationship is that, whereas the second building inherited the *physical* foundation stone of the first Goetheanum, the new *social* organism of the Anthroposophical Society

received a 'foundation stone' in the form of a set of mantric verses, known as The Foundation Stone Meditation. The intention of this latter foundation stone was to sustain anthroposophical work anywhere in the 'temple' of the earth itself.

3 References to 'theosophy' in Steiner's early lecture can be understood in the same way as 'anthroposophy' ('wisdom of the human being'), a term he coined after he left the Theosophical Society (see chapter 6, note 2).

4 'Great epoch' is used here to describe a much larger sweep of time that encompasses all the smaller cultural epochs Steiner subsequently goes on to list.

5 See chapter 3, note 1.

6 A sculpture group from antiquity that shows the priest Laocoon and his two sons being squeezed to death by serpents.

7 This is a shorthand reference to a process, which Steiner describes elsewhere, by which disharmony in the astral body, or soul, can be channelled into the physical body via the etheric body. See also chapter 2, note 2.

8 This may refer to the idea that the seventh stage involves the total transformation of the physical body, which in fact 'overthrows' it at a physical level, rendering it supersensible.

9 Elohim is the Hebrew name for one of the nine heirarchies of spiritual beings as understood in Judaeo–Christian literature. The Elohim are also known as Spirits of Form. They gave form to the human body and created the self.

Sources

Chapter 1
30 December 1914, in *Art as Seen in the Light of Mystery Wisdom*, pp. 50–51
29 December 1914, in *Art as Seen in the Light of Mystery Wisdom*, pp. 32–5
2 January 1915, in *Art as Seen in the Light of Mystery Wisdom*, pp. 115–16

Chapter 2
14 September 1907, in *Occult Signs and Symbols*, pp. 15–21

Chapter 3
4 August 1908, in *Universe Earth and Man*, pp. 15–16, 17–18, 18–19
17 June 1914, in *Architecture as a Synthesis of the Arts*, pp. 84–7
4 August 1908, in *Universe Earth and Man*, pp. 20–21

Chapter 4
28 June 1914, in *Architecture as a Synthesis of the Arts*, pp. 99–111, 111–15

Chapter 5
7 June 1914, in *Architecture as a Synthesis of the Arts*, pp. 55–68

Chapter 6
Text from folder, October 1907. Translation by Rex Raab
4th January 1915, in *Art as Seen in the Light of Mystery Wisdom*, pp. 145–54

Chapter 7
2 January 1915, in *Art as Seen in the Light of Mystery Wisdom*, pp. 116–18

7 June 1914, in *Architecture as a Synthesis of the Arts*, pp. 68–9

17 June 1914, in *Architecture as a Synthesis of the Arts*, pp. 81–2, 89–91, 94–5

Talk given at the dedication of the new Building for Anthroposophy in Stuttgart, 15 October 1911 (typescript).

Chapter 8
Illustrated talk given in The Hague, 28 February 1921 (typescript)

Chapter 9
1 November 1924, article in *Die National-Zeitung* newspaper, published in *Architecture as a Synthesis of the Arts*, pp. 173–6

Chapter 10
23 January 1914, in *Architecture as a Synthesis of the Arts*, pp. 35–49

Chapter 11
12 December 1911, in *Architecture as a Synthesis of the Arts*, pp. 3–20

Chapter 12
15 May 1905, in *The Temple Legend*, pp. 121–35

Bibliography

Books by Rudolf Steiner:

Art as Seen in the Light of Mystery Wisdom, Rudolf Steiner Press 1984
Occult Signs and Symbols, Anthroposophic Press 1972
Universe, Earth and Man, Rudolf Steiner Press 1955
Architecture as a Synthesis of the Arts, Rudolf Steiner Press 1999
The Temple Legend and the Golden Legend, Rudolf Steiner Press 2002
An Outline of Esoteric Science, Anthroposophic Press 1997
From Jesus to Christ, Rudolf Steiner Press 1973
Manifestations of Karma, Rudolf Steiner Press 1995

Typescripts:

Talk given at the dedication of the new building for anthroposophy in Stuttgart, 15 October 1911
Text from folder, October 1907, translated by Rex Raab
Illustrated talk given in The Hague, 28 February 1921

Books by other authors:

Biesantz, Hagen, and Klingborg, Arne, *The Goetheanum – Rudolf Steiner's Architectural Impulse*, Rudolf Steiner Press 1979
Blundell-Jones, Peter, *Hans Scharoun*, Phaidon, London, 1995
Colquhoun, Alan, *Modern Architecture*, Oxford University Press 2002

Colquhoun, Margaret, and Ewald, Axel, *New Eyes For Plants*, Hawthorn Press 1996

Fant, A., Klingborg, A., and Wilkes, J., *Rudolf Steiner's Sculpture*, Rudolf Steiner Press 1975

Grosse, Rudolf, *The Christmas Foundation – Beginning of a New Cosmic Age*, Anthroposophic Press (no date given)

Le Corbusier, *The Modulor – A Harmonious Measure to the Human Scale Universally Applicable to Architecture and Mechanics*, Faber and Faber, 1951

Mees, L.F.C., *Secrets of the Skeleton – Form in Metamorphosis*, Anthroposophic Press 1984

Pehnt, Wolfgang, *Expressionist Architecture*, Thames and Hudson 1973

Schwenk, T., *Sensitive Chaos – The Creation of Flowing Forms in Water and Air*, Rudolf Steiner Press 1965

Sharp, Dennis, *Modern Architecture and Expressionism*, Longmans 1966

Thompson, D'Arcy W., *On Growth and Form*, Cambridge University Press, 1966

Tuchman, Maurice, et al., *The Spiritual in Art: Abstract Painting 1890–1985*, Los Angeles County Museum of Art & Abbeville Press, New York, 1986 (exhibition catalogue with supporting essays)

Further Reading

General

Bayes, Kenneth, *Living Architecture*, Floris Books, Edinburgh, 1994. A general introduction to Steiner's work and comparison with other approaches to architecture in the twentieth century.

Biezantz, Hagen, and Klingborg, Arne, etc., *The Goetheanum – Rudolf Steiner's Architectural Impulse*, Rudolf Steiner Press, London, 1979. Out of print.

Blaser, Werner, *Nature in Building – Rudolf Steiner in Dornach 1913–25*, Birkhäuser 2002

First Goetheanum

Fant, Ake, Klingborg, Arne, and Wilkes, John, *Rudolf Steiner's Sculpture*, Rudolf Steiner Press, London, 1975. A comprehensively illustrated account of the 'Group' sculpture intended for the first Goetheanum. Out of print.

Raske, Hilde, *The Language of Color in the First Goetheanum – A Study of Rudolf Steiner's Art*, Walter Keller Verlag, Dornach, Switzerland, 1983. A comprehensive account of the paintings on the ceilings of the two domes, illustrated by reproductions of Steiner's working sketches, and including extracts from lectures on the themes that the paintings illustrate.

Second Goetheanum

Pehnt, Wolfgang, *Rudolf Steiners Goetheanum, Dornach*, Ernst & Sohn 1991

Raab, Rex, Klingborg, Arne, and Fant, Ake, *Eloquent Concrete*, Rudolf Steiner Press, London, 1979. Out of print.

Various authors, *The Great Hall of the Goetheanum – Its Completion at the End of the Century*, Special English Edition of *Stil* magazine, Arts Section of the School of Spiritual Sceince, 1994. A specialist journal, available from Art Section, c/o Christian Thal-Jantzen, Mulberry House, 16 Hoathly Hill, West Hoathly, West Sussex, RH19 4SJ. A series of illustrated articles on artistic questions connected with the translation of Steiner's designs for elements from the interior of the first Goetheanum into an appropriate expression for the interior of the second Goetheanum.

Goethean Science

Naydler, Jeremy, Ed., *Goethe on Science, An Anthology of Goethe's Scientific Writings*, Floris Books, Edinburgh, 1996

By Steiner:

Nature's Open Secret – Introductions to Goethe's Scientific Works, Anthroposophic Press. A collection of Steiner's introductions to chapters in a comprehensive edition of Goethe's scientific writings, published in 1882.

By others:

Bortoft, Henri, *The Wholeness of Nature – Goethe's Way of Science*, Floris Books, Edinburgh, 1996. A comprehensive overview of Goethe's scientific method.

Illustration Credits

Pages 4, 102–4, 106–8, 158, 164–5, 167: Rudolf Kemper, *Der Bau*, 1966; pages 101, 127, 131, 148, 160, 166, 168, 191: Biesantz and Klingborg, *The Goetheanum, Rudolf Steiner's Architectural Impulse*, Rudolf Steiner Press, 1979; page 5: ed. Aline B. Saarinen, *Eero Saarinen on his Work*, Yale, 1962; page 6: Le Corbusier, *The Modulor*, 2nd ed., Faber, 1951; page 8: Peter Blundell-Jones, *Hans Scharoun*, Phaidon, London, 1995; page 24: Hilde Raske, *The Language of Color in the First Goetheanum, A Study of Rudolf Steiner's Art*, Walter Keller Verlag, Dornach, Switzerland, 1983; page 217–8: ed. Henri Stierlin, *Architecture of the World, Egypt*, Taschen, undated; pages 25, 41: ed. Henri Stierlin, *Architecture of the World, Greece*, Taschen, undated; pages 30, 48, 220: ed. Henri Stierlin, *Architecture of the World, Gothic*, Taschen, undated; page 41, Bannister-Fletcher, ed. John Musgrove, *A History of Architecture*, 19th ed., Butterworths, 1987; pages 55, 59, 60, 63, 65, 66, 67, 71, 72, 79, 81, 82, 83, 84, 86, 87, 88, 89, 90, 91, 95, 114, 130, 181, 186: Rudolf Steiner, ed. Christian Thal-Jantzen, *Architecture as a Synthesis of the Arts*, Rudolf Steiner Press, 1999; pages 57, 73, 110, 153, 155, 157, 161, 162, 169, 171, 173, 179: ed. Walter Roggenkamp, *Das Goetheanum, als Gesamtkunstwerk*, Verlag am Goetheanum, 1986; pages 117, 122, 178, 194–5, 198, 200, 207: Rex Raab, Arne Kingborg, Ake Fant, *Eloquent Concrete*, Rudolf Steiner Press, London, 1979; page 129: *Stil*, magazine, 2/1998; page 136: Assya Turgeniev, *The Goetheanum Windows*, Rudolf Steiner Pub. Co., 1938; pages 175–7: John Wilkes, *Rudolf Steiner's Sculpture*, Rudolf Steiner Press; pages 202, 204, 208: Wolfgang Pehnt, *Rudolf Steiner's*

Goetheanum, Dornach, Ernst & Sohn, 1991; pages 39, 224: S. Giedion, *The Eternal Present, The Beginnings of Architecture*, Oxford, 1964; pages 115, 119, 120: *Art As Seen in the Light of Mystery Wisdom*, Rudolf Steiner Press, 1996; pages 50–1, 184, 219, 226: from the editor's collection.

Note Regarding Rudolf Steiner's Lectures

The lectures and addresses contained in this volume have been translated from the German, which is based on stenographic and other recorded texts that were in most cases never seen or revised by the lecturer. Hence, due to human errors in hearing and transcription, they may contain mistakes and faulty passages. Every effort has been made to ensure that this is not the case. Some of the lectures were given to audiences more familiar with anthroposophy; these are the so-called 'private' or 'members' lectures. Other lectures, like the written works, were intended for the general public. The difference between these, as Rudolf Steiner indicates in his *Autobiography*, is twofold. On the one hand, the members' lectures take for granted a background in and commitment to anthroposophy; in the public lectures this was not the case. At the same time, the members' lectures address the concerns and dilemmas of the members, while the public work speaks directly out of Steiner's own understanding of universal needs. Nevertheless, as Rudolf Steiner stresses: 'Nothing was ever said that was not solely the result of my direct experience of the growing content of anthroposophy. There was never any question of concessions to the prejudices and preferences of the members. Whoever reads these privately printed lectures can take them to represent anthroposophy in the fullest sense. Thus it was possible without hesitation—when the complaints in this direction became too persistent—to depart from the custom of circulating this material "For members only". But it must be borne in mind that faulty passages do occur in these reports not revised by myself.' Earlier in the same chapter, he states: 'Had I been able to correct them [the private lectures], the restriction *for members only* would have been unnecessary from the beginning.'

The original German editions on which this text is based were published by Rudolf Steiner Verlag, Dornach, Switzerland in the collected edition (*Gesamtausgabe*, 'GA') of Rudolf Steiner's work. All publications are edited by the Rudolf Steiner Nachlassverwaltung (estate), which wholly owns both Rudolf Steiner Verlag and the Rudolf Steiner Archive. The organization relies solely on donations to continue its activity.

For further information please contact:

Rudolf Steiner Archiv
Postfach 135
CH-4143 Dornach

or:

www.rudolf-steiner.com

ALSO AVAILABLE IN THE SAME SERIES:

AGRICULTURE

Compiled with an introduction, commentary and notes by
Richard Thornton Smith

The evolving human being; Cosmos as the source of life; Plants
and the living earth; Farms and the realms of nature; Bringing
the chemical elements to life; Soil and the world of spirit;
Supporting and regulating life processes; Spirits of the elements;
Nutrition and vitality; Responsibility for the future

ISBN 1 85584 113 4

ART

Compiled with an introduction, commentary and notes by Anne Stockton

The being of the arts; Goethe as the founder of a new science of aesthetics; Technology and art; At the turn of each new millennium; The task of modern art and architecture; The living walls; The glass windows; Colour on the walls; Form—moving the circle; The seven planetary capitals of the first Goetheanum; The model and the statue 'The Representative of Man'; Colour and faces; Physiognomies

ISBN 1 85584 138 X

EDUCATION

Compiled with an introduction, commentary and notes by
Christopher Clouder

A social basis for education; The spirit of the Waldorf school; Educational methods based on anthroposophy; The child at play; Teaching from a foundation of spiritual insight and education in the light of spiritual science; The adolescent after the fourteenth year; Science, art, religion and morality; The spiritual grounds of education; The role of caring in education; The roots of education and the kingdom of childhood; Address at a parents' evening; Education in the wider social context

ISBN 1 85584 118 5

MEDICINE

Compiled with an introduction, commentary and notes by
Andrew Maendl, MB, BS

Understanding man's true nature as a basis for medical practice;
The science of knowing; The mission of reverence; The four
temperaments; The bridge between universal spirituality and the
physical; The constellation of the supersensible bodies; The
invisible human within us: the pathology underlying therapy;
Cancer and mistletoe, and aspects of psychiatry; Case history
questions: diagnosis and therapy; Anthroposophical medicine in
practice: three case histories

ISBN 1 85584 133 9

RELIGION

Compiled with an introduction, commentary and notes by
Andrew Welburn

Mysticism and beyond: the importance of prayer; The meaning of sin and grace; Rediscovering the Bible; What is true communion?; Rediscovering the festivals and the life of the earth; Finding one's destiny: walking with Christ; The significance of religion in life and death; Christ's second coming: the truth for our time; Universal religion: the meaning of love

ISBN 1 85584 128 2

SCIENCE

Compiled with an introduction, commentary and notes by
Howard Smith

From pre-science to science; The origin of mathematics; The roots of physics and chemistry, and the urge to experiment; Are there limits to what science can know?; Understanding organisms: Goethe's method; The quest for archetypal phenomena; Light, darkness and colour; The rediscovery of the elements; What is warmth?; The scale of nature; The working of the ethers in the physical; Sub-nature; What are atoms?; Natural science and spiritual science

ISBN 1 85584 108 8

SOCIAL AND POLITICAL SCIENCE

Compiled with an introduction, commentary and notes by
Stephen E. Usher

Psychological cognition; The social question; The social question and theosophy; Memoranda of 1917; The metamorphosis of intelligence; Culture, law and economy; Central Europe between East and West

ISBN 1 85584 103 7